Red Dust

JORDAN VALLEY DUST

Red Dust

A Classic Account of
Australian Light Horsemen
in Palestine During the
First World War

Donald Black

LEONAUR

Red Dust: a Classic Account of Australian Light Horsemen
in Palestine During the First World War
by Donald Black

Published by Leonaur Ltd

ISBN: 978-1-84677-484-3 (hardcover)
ISBN: 978-1-84677-483-6 (softcover)

http://www.leonaur.com

Publisher's Notes

The opinions expressed in this book are those of the author
and are not necessarily those of the publisher.

Contents

Beersheba and After 9

The Raid 29

Rum, Whisky, Wine & Bad Women 47

O' Jerusalem 60

Into the Jordan Valley 70

Across the Jordan 81

Assault on the Plateau 96

Life in the Valley 112

Out of the Line 122

Cairo 131

Ride Out to Conquer 160

A handful of dust made animate by blood to struggle with fate through life's allotted span, then to the dust again from which all life sprang.

Soldiers, what are they?
Just dust, red dust.

To friend and foe and the imperishable memory of lost comrades, hoping their sacrifice will not be in vain, but will serve as the rock foundations of the tabernacle of better understanding between the nations. And in tribute to our comrades-in-arms, the gallant Tommy infantrymen whose heroic conduct made possible the greatest cavalry feat the world has known.

Chapter 1

Beersheba and After

At last the wearily monotonous desert campaign, with its waterless sands and burning skies, has drawn to a close. We knock at the portals of Palestine, in our ever onward surge. Twice have we essayed to gain a footing at its gateway, twice we have been repulsed. Once we had penetrated into the Turks' very citadel, Gaza itself, only to leave the half-held prize. Now we lie in a *wadi* nearby, awaiting the third attempt which rumour, that forerunner of truth, predicts as imminent.

For eighteen months the campaign has dragged on amongst the sands, starting with the Turks' disastrous attempt to cross the canal in boats; from then he has been slowly forced back.

Through the centuries armies have fought up and down the Sinai peninsula with Gaza as the stepping-off stone both to and from the desert. Still extant evidences of past battles constantly remind us of this. Not the least noticeable are the mis-coloured polls of some of the Arabs. It is most unusual to see a red or curly headed Arab: the fact that we have seen a number along the desert seaboard tells of many an affair Napoleonic soldiers have had with the local native women.

Still once again the enemy lies without, ready to pounce on this key town like a dog on a bone. The desert with its ever-changing sands has been a dreary battlefield. A series of pitched encounters along its edge has brought us nearer and nearer, till now we are at the gateway.

The desert has been a hard master; it offers little and demands much; the water is scattered and the only shelter, an occasional *hod*. The continual glare and heat with numerous sandstorms and the endless sameness have made the task more difficult.

We look forward to Palestine, where we will be rid of these things and feel firm ground beneath our feet. The desert has been mostly guerilla warfare. Attempts to dig trenches were usually abortive, as the sand would pour back almost as quickly as we dug it. The transport had been fitted with extra-wide wheel tyres to gain a purchase on the slipping sands. Pneumatic-tyred motors had been useless, until it was found that wire-netting made an excellent roadway when pegged to the sand. The heavy sand had broken many of our horses and shortage of food developed in them all a depraved taste. They would nibble at anything, even their tails and manes, and often nosed amongst their droppings for undigested grain. Through this their bellies became filled with sand.

A wounded man in the desert knew a kind of hell, peculiar to the modes of transport that the exigencies of the country made necessary. The sand cart with its wire-mattress flooring gave a small degree of comfort, but even here the inevitable jerking over sand hills caused agonies, which however were light compared with those of the cacolets, which were two chairs in which a man could lie slung one each side of a camel. The camel has a rolling gait that moves these chairs with a jerky action, inflicting hellish torture upon the wounded. Many died of it; but nothing better could be devised to serve the conditions; so it was a chance whether a man died of his wounds or the transport.

Despite the added hardships which the desert has heaped upon us, it holds a fascination which, to those who have dwelt upon it, will never quite dim. Its magnetism will always leave a memory.

Sleeping in the open, with at most only a canvas covering overhead, one sees and feels the nearness of nature. The stars at night appear very low in the heavens, and many an hour we whiled away gazing up at them. We come very close to nature in the desert, not only in our surroundings but in our living and habits.

All this is now finished; we are like the Israelites who have passed through the wilderness and approach the land of milk and honey - but the milk and honey have long since dried up.

The double failure at Gaza has had far reaching results; they are too disastrous efforts, as the many mute graves testify. The Turk believes himself impregnable in this fortress, with its long-range naval guns and heavy emplacements. We were unable to drag the heavy artillery necessary over the sands and resorted to monitors instead. The numerous ruins bear witness to the accuracy of their bombardment.

The whole scheme of attack is to be altered. The line is being strengthened with heavier guns and many more planes. Hordes of infantry are pouring in, everything points to a very determined third attempt. Rumours usually carry more than a semblance of truth, and this one apparently is no exception. Indications are that it will be a long and bitter struggle.

The term rumour is one we seldom use, preferring the less polite but more expressive 'Latrine Wireless.' It is nearly always from these places that stories emanate. It is but natural that men grouped together as they are, when attending to nature's very vital urging, will discuss matters of importance to themselves; usually it is our future movements. The latrines become a sort of news exchange. One constantly hears it said 'I heard in a latrine, so and so is likely to happen'; or it may be put 'Have you heard the latest wireless?'

* * * * * * * *

The line has been quiet for weeks with a quietness that grows ominous. We have been occupying a *wadi* bed, providing patrols and outposts, keeping a watchful eye on the territory intervening between the Turks and ourselves. Daily growing lousier and dirtier, whilst preparations go on apace.

Our time expired, we move to the seaboard to refit and make ready. Our days are fully occupied; a mounted man has little to spare at any time, even when resting. The horses keep him constantly busy; still, we find time to swim each day, which is a boon beyond words. We manage time to delouse, a very necessary operation, always attended to when resting, but of little use in the line. Lice are picked up again as quickly as destroyed.

Cavalry always work in sections of fours. Our rations too are issued in this manner. When in action on foot, one holds the horses of the other three. What one has, we all have; we are as four brothers.

We have the troop machine-gun in our section. This gives us added duties. Stone and Banks sit by it now, cleaning and oiling. Hill, the remaining member of the section, is busy killing lice.

The sand hills here are alive with desert dogs, a pariah akin to the wolf. They come near the lines at nights, creating a bedlam with their piercingly blood-curdling yells. Often we take our rifles and shoot at them by the light of the moon.

All is very quiet and peaceful by the beach; we are far removed from the front line. We seldom hear any gunfire, and nothing occurs to disturb our rest, so we laze, at peace with all. Hardly do we realise that but a little while ago we were the centre of a maelstrom; with the fatalism that war seems to breed, we think of the future, worrying little.

We know that the coming offensive will be on a larger scale than those of the past. The command of the front has changed hands, bringing General Allenby, skilled in the use of cavalry, which will take us to the fore when the advance occurs, but that is of the future, it can care for itself.

We live in the present, for the present. Death is always so near, one never knows when its icy hand will reach forth. We have seen so many go and live in half expectation of following; it seems as if the war will never reach an end. The longer we live the more we fear, seeing friends go makes us wonder who will be next.

We talk little of home; letters come and we write back; but home is so far away and so many there are who left it what seems a lifetime ago. It is doubtful if we will survive till peace, home seems to be in a life we have lived in another world. We feel almost as disassociated beings, lost in a whirlpool, from which there is no escape in life. Though we long for the time

WATER TROUGHS AT KHAN JUNIS NEAR SHEIKH NURAN

CAMEL CACOLET FOR CARRYING WOUNDED

when perhaps we will escape and return, an armistice seems the least likely thing to happen.

****

From the beach we move into supports, some miles inland, in readiness for the anticipated advance. A forsaken place it is and we curse the gods who made it. A desolation, surely created when the Almighty powers were seething in rage. The ground is of a loose heavy dust formation, with patches of outcropping gravelly earth. Dotted about here and there is a sort of stunted grass root, or an occasional tree, drooping under the weight of dust blown upon it. The only life, a few mangy natives living in mud huts, eking out an exceedingly precarious livelihood from God only knows what. No sign of eatable vegetation exists. The country seems given over to pests: rats living in field burrows, scorpions, snakes.

The rats burrow over large areas, like rabbits, to ride or walk over which risks a broken leg. The scorpions give us hell, the doctor is always treating bites - usually by injections, which bring about fainting, during which the poison seems to subside. With the little scarabs we are on more friendly terms, and they supply a source of constant amusement.

We often lie for hours with a couple of these little fellows and watch them roll great balls of horse-dung about, betting on which of a number will get his lump a certain distance first. At night-time we like them less, they awaken us by crawling over our bellies. Blankets have always to be shaken free of these little creatures each night. They crawl amongst the folds during the day.

The rats are a far greater annoyance at night. When we are lying asleep, dreaming perhaps, they scamper across our naked flesh, often two and three times in a night. No amount of pegging down the sides of our shelters will keep them out. They seem to like the human stink and will burrow in. Nothing creeps the blood like a rat crawling over naked flesh, the shudder remains for minutes after the rat has gone. Sometimes we find snakes in our blankets, deadly little fellows of the viper breed.

14

We are some two miles from water and have to ride through the loose dust, which rises up in clouds, enveloping us, so that our mouths and eyes and nose become full of it. In the morning the air is still, towards afternoon the wind rises, blowing the dust everywhere. We see it coming like a huge cloud, rolling along the ground. We then seek the shelter of our bivouacs till it passes, but usually it blows for two hours with almost clock-like precision.

The horses stand with their heads bowed and tails towards it, poor miserable creatures, they have no shelters. The afternoon watering takes place at its height and those unlucky ones whose turn it is, creep out and ride away in a long half-blinded line. Constantly the dust will close our eyes so that we cannot see where we are riding and let the horses walk on the heels of those in front. Sometimes a man is kicked and rolls off into the dust, to grovel till the pain subsides.

★ ★ ★ ★ ★ ★ ★ ★

We stand ready by our horses, awaiting the word to mount and move off. The wheel turns on, the gathering clouds are breaking. The night will be very dark; it is always when there is no moon that we ride. The last rays of light are passing as we form the column and ride into the night. For hours we ride, not a word is spoken, not a cigarette glows. The only sound the chink of bits and the low swishing of hooves on the ground; occasionally varied by the click of a kicked stone, or a whispered word as an order is passed along. The country ahead is unfriendly, so we ride in silence. Each hour we stop a few minutes to rest the horses, then silently mount and move on again. As time passes we walk and ride alternately to save our mounts. The craving for a cigarette grows, but we dare not smoke. Under our hat bands we have holes burned and during the halts one can lie full length with the hat flat in front and smoke through the opening; in this way not even those near can see.

We pass some wells without a halt; the march is forced and minutes count. It is the only watering place about, but the horses are still fresh and can wait till morning. On we go through the

15

dark, marching by the stars. Sometimes we lose touch and have to canter forward, sometimes we stray from the column as our brains numb with the incessant call of sleep.

Just before sunrise we reach the end of the first stage, a deserted settlement where it is intended to remain for the day till the friendly pall of night comes again to envelope us.

The Turk has anticipated us and blown up the wells. We work frantically on them till the sun is sinking but without avail. Half the column goes back to the wells we passed in the night. Another day dawns and still no water. Our bottles are empty and the horses grow restless. We search and find a few holes which yield enough for a drink but no more, still the horses thirst. Another day passes before the wells are opened and water flows. The thirsty horses drink their fill and we get enough for two drinks, but none for washing.

Night falls and once again that snake-like column, an hour's ride long, merges into the dark and is eaten up by the shadows. The light is failing as the head leads out, it is black darkness when the last man moves.

We divide into two columns, horsemen in one, transport, guns, etc. in the other. We move quickly, the Turk knows of our occupation of the wells but expects a longer delay. We hope to arrive and catch him unprepared.

We ride in silence, hurriedly, every man anticipating, silently communing with his thoughts. Dawn will bring death to many, we know, but to whom?

With daylight we draw near. The column divides into detachments, like so many arrows, ready to speed on the town (Beersheba) ahead. Spreading out, we ride like hawks on the fold, expected, but not so soon. Squadrons tear by, men with their heads low, their faces tense. Bits of equipment come adrift and fly away. No one stays to get them. Someone says enough gear is lost to equip a regiment.

Despite the suddenness of our appearance the Turk fights stubbornly till almost dark. Shells whine and burst overhead. Our artillery bombards the town but still they resist, till one regiment charges them on horseback, almost a forlorn hope, a desperate measure to get the town before dark and as desperate efforts so often are, it is successful.

* * * * * * * *

A day passes in clearing the country, gathering prisoners and breaking through so as to cut across to the coast. Our brigade advances along the main highway towards Dhaheriya, in an endeavour to come in behind. The fighting is close up and nasty, mostly from ridge to ridge amongst the short gullies between the hills.

Our squadron pulls in behind a ridge and prepares to throw a line of outposts along its crest for the night. We have a new hand in the section; Hill was killed this morning, feeding the gun; his brother too had his thigh shattered. I feel his loss, for we had always bivouacked together. When the nights were cold we used to lie with our bodies close to gain warmth. One misses these friends, they are more than brothers. I have his little personal things; I took them from his dead body, still warm with the blood flowing from his splintered head.

It is not yet dark and we are hungry, only a few biscuits in the last twenty-four hours. We have a little water and some cocoa; we mix this and heat it but have neither sugar nor milk. It is not very pleasant tasting but warms our vitals against the cold night closing down upon us.

Brent takes our horses, links his arm through the bridle reins and lies down, hoping to sleep. He has come in place of Hill. Stone holds three varying length straws to decide which shift each will take. I draw the first and prepare for my lonely vigil, whilst the other two roll over to rest.

Wriggling to the top of the ridge I adjust the gun and set the ammunition panniers in a V formation in front, feed a strip in and charge the breach. This done I make myself as comfortable as possible, unable to remove the quantity of impedimenta slung about me.

The cold of the night is already penetrating through my clothes. I have a pair of socks over my hands like gloves and swathe my overcoat around me to the best advantage. Taking my night-glasses I commence scanning the terrain ahead, my eyes gradually becoming used to the darkness.

I am feeling very weary, the first effects of the ardours of the past days. It is at this stage the brain commences playing tricks, causing one to see imaginary things. The nervous strain creates hallucinations, so that one has constant visions of non-existent things moving about in the dark ahead.

It is a common complaint, we all get it, and learn to expect these tricks of our brains when the night draws on and darkness envelopes us as we lie, gazing into a void straining our eyes in search of movement. The constant peering into the night works on our brains, so that we imagine we see that for which we seek. Suddenly it vanishes and we trouble to know if anything had really been there, or if it was only the *willies* as we term it.

I have been watching a bush, uncertain if it is a bush; it seems to change its shape, as men do who sit and become cramped. It may be an enemy outpost, the distance is too great to be sure. I move my eyes around to the left and for a few minutes keep them away from the bush, then turning back again I find the bush is no longer there.

I think of firing a burst into it but that may result in anything happening, so I just continue to watch and keep my gun trained that way.

Something appears in the corner of my eye. I look round. It is undoubtedly moving. It is low down and moving at an incline, so that I am not sure of its speed, but it is definitely coming nearer, very low like a man crawling on his belly.

I change my glasses to the left hand and hold my revolver in my right. My ribs ache from this cramped position but I cannot move for fear of attracting attention.

Turning my head I see the bush is still there, I draw a bead on it with the gun and know it has not moved. Leaving the gun I again pay attention to the moving something. It definitely is alive but what it is I cannot tell.

It stops and for a minute I imagine I am seeing things, then it moves again and to my ears comes a blood-curdling howl. My heart stands still, the very blood seeming to turn to ice in my veins, then goes pumping away again as I realise it is a desert dog. I shudder involuntarily as I relax.

Had I lain behind the line somewhere this cry would have had no effect. It is lying here alone, with nerves keyed up. A shell would have made less impression.

From behind me comes a snore, I move back and kick Banks in the ribs, he grunts and is quiet. Listening intently I can hear the champ of bits, we dare not remove these from the horses.

Sleep is weighing down on me; it gets increasingly difficult to keep awake. I pinch myself till it hurts, but it is little help, I even bump my head against the gun. I long to walk about, to stretch my legs but at most can only wriggle my body a little. Peering into the dark acts like self-hypnosis and aggravates tiredness the more.

The biting cold has numbed my fingers and toes and I feel clumsy and awkward. I try to hold the gun trigger but my finger slips about the guard.

* * * * * * *

Looking at my watch I see three hours have passed, my shift is ended. Crawling back a little I waken Stone. He growlingly takes my place. I stay a little with him to be sure he is properly awake then roll to rest.

It seems I have not been asleep at all when I am awakened by kicks in the ribs. It is the zero hour, the dread stand-to. I feel it is useless to stand up when I can sit in comfort here. I close my eyes, may as well rest them, no use sitting up gaping, I will not go to sleep again and can rest this way. Again I feel the battering in the ribs and hear the sergeant cursing.

When light comes we mount our horses and ride on, with empty bellies and dry tongues. Some stray Turks offer themselves as prisoners but we chase them away. They would only be a hindrance and put an added strain on our rations, none too plentiful when we have them. The infantry coming behind can have them, we bequeath them the full honour of their capture.

19

Towards afternoon we come across a convoy of lorries carrying infantry. As we watch them from a distance we see an ambush sprung by the roadside. Two armoured cars rush towards it, their machine-guns spattering as they go. The engine of one stalls, a figure creeps out from the cabin and swings the handle; it takes guts to do that.

We swing around and above the ambush and charge down the roadway towards it. We catch the enfilading fire but we serve our purpose. The cars seeing their advantage press into it, and we become encumbered with a batch of unwanted prisoners.

The Squadron Leader interviews the infantry commander and points out the impossibility of our retaining them, we are mounted and cannot lag behind with foot prisoners. Either he takes them or we must disarm them, leave them to roam the country and later be collected. The infantryman decides to relieve us of them. What he does with them is his worry; we have rid ourselves of the encumbrance and gallop on.

Towards late afternoon we ride into the town for water. The thought of it makes us eager, we are now practically speechless with thirst and though we long to smoke we cannot, we are too dry. I feel a sort of gnawing feeling internally, like rats; it is want of food.

A small Turkish railway engine has been blown bodily off the line by one of our shells. It lies near to the wells. The engineers have succeeded, in their usual amazing way into persuading it to resume action as a pump.

Around the troughs are line after line of mounted men with their horses, taking their turn to water, those behind fighting their thirst-crazed horses to keep them from clearing all in front as they smell the water. Poor dumb beasts, theirs is the greater suffering, they know not what it is for; they have been brought into the war as so much equipment, whereas we have come of our own free will, knowing or thinking we knew to what end, with our eyes open.

Our detachment waters, and moves out; it is the first drink our horses have had for sixty hours. Sixty hours of galloping and charging under the cruelly sweating sun. Their sides are shrunken and their eyes bloodshot.

I stay behind with Brent to help him with Tom the pack-horse, who is a bit fractious. This temporary separation from the troop gives us an opportunity to forage. Search as we do, little is to be found, only some dried sheet apricots I take from some Turkish dead. The corner of one piece is stained red, we tear it off and wolf the remainder, greedy that we waste even a corner.

We are not concerned much about the source of this food. We would cheerfully take it out of a dead man's mouth, or rob the angel Gabriel himself; we are hungry indeed.

* * * * * * * *

As the friendly coat of the night's darkness lifts, the day comes hot and red, with a redness about the sun that presages ill for many.

Through the boiling heat of the day we chase the Turk from ridge to ridge, never quite catching him. We come across a deserted Turkish field bakery and find hundreds of little black loaves. We seize these eagerly; they are manna from heaven, even if sun-dried. Some tea too, in bags, is quickly snatched up. We have eaten our iron ration days ago, and this is the first food I have had in thirty hours.

Towards mid-afternoon the evenness of the plain country changes as we enter a rocky formation, with small cliffs and knolls. Ideal to ambush a pursuer in, ideal to wreak havoc on a fleeing enemy.

It was a matter of who seized the natural advantage of the country first. Both seemed to realise the possibilities at once, for the Turk is making the most stubborn resistance since Beersheba.

Our troop, to gain a hill, goes galloping ahead through a veritable leaden hail. We reach the ridge, but so heavy is the machine-gun fire, that we can neither move forward nor raise our heads to use the position. We breathe our horses then gallop to a lateral hill, which gives us command of those withstanding us.

Coming to this second rise we find many enemy dead and dying, but the position is too urgent to aid them. A few resist as we dismount to man the ridge. The action is so close that it is impossible to use our rifles, we thrust at them with our bayonets like a short sword and leave them lying, to add their cries to the others already here.

I linger behind Stone and Banks to get the extra ammunition panniers and buckle up the pack. Whilst I am occupied by this a small body of the enemy round a corner nearby and are quickly accounted for.

One comes up behind me as I buckle the panniers. I am unaware of his presence till Smith, rushing by, runs him through as he passes, toppling him over against me. We both fall in a heap, the Turk with his slit belly squirting his life's blood over me. I jump up a little dazed but feeling nothing, pick up my panniers and rush up the hill, a gory mess.

From the ridge the country opens out before us. Immediately in front and below is a gully with an orchard, the first we have seen, on its far side, not three hundred yards away. Rushing through the fruit trees, in hundreds, are Turks, apparently pursued from behind.

Such a target seldom offers to a machine-gunner, it is almost cowardly to fire on them, but it is very necessary that we do. Should they find cover they are in sufficient strength to provide formidable opposition.

Stone lies working the gun, Banks feeding it with feverish speed. I throw them the full panniers and start loading the empty strips. The little Hotchkiss is pounding away at six hundred rounds a minute. The barrel runs hot, Banks in his excitement to change it forgets his leather gloves and burns his hands. I take his place till the pain subsides. He sits behind us holding his hands and cursing.

Our ammunition runs low, we collect the bandoliers from the troop, empty the clips and refill the gun strips. Still the Turks pour through the orchard. They are like sheep, brainless in their insane desire to escape what follows them and heedless in their craziness of the fate overtaking them as our gun pours devastation amongst them.

Their mad rush dies away, our gun stops. Through the comparative silence, the temporary lull in the firing changes to agonised cries, audible to us across the gully. The cries of the wounded mingle with those of the dying.

One becomes to a degree inured to bloodshed and slaughter, but no matter how much of it we see, there are times when even the most hardened feel nauseated. Such is opposite us now.

We have little time to dwell on this catastrophe; a flight of our planes passes over. We have advanced so much since the morning that we are mistaken for the enemy. The airmen drop their bombs on us. We are unable to let them know their mistake; we can only find what shelter we can and shrink away from the flying fragments.

They pass on, leaving casualties amongst us. Night is falling and we are not yet at the pumping station. It is imperative we take this all important place, as success depends on our holding the water supply there.

In the distance we can hear the guns, whilst much ahead of our previous position, rifles and machine guns are hammering away; the advance goes on apace. A gun-carriage, part of the Somerset battery, thunders past not far away, drawn by its eight sweating and foam-flecked horses, whilst in its wake comes a detachment of Warwickshire Yeomen, swords in hand, moving at the gallop. They have done good work today these Warwicks. We watched them around midday, charge the very muzzles of a belching enemy battery and take it too, then continue their mad career onwards. Good men and brave!

Coming down from the ridge top, we do what we can for the Turks lying at its base, those we had encountered as we galloped in. I see the one Smith ran through; he is lying on his side with one arm out-flung, the other curled under him. He is quite dead, his clothes sodden and a little pool near by from the blood let out of his belly.

* * * * * * * *

How good the water smells! It is forty-eight hours since last the horses drank. We are little better off, our mouths are dry and cracked. My tongue feels like a piece of rough paper, it is like a file.

23

RAILWAY STATION AT BEERSHEBA

TURKS WATCH THE BATTLE OF SHERIA (GERMAN PHOTOGRAPH)

The horses, poor creatures, are sunken in the belly, their heads hanging, suffering torture but still willing to carry us. I stroke Blackboy's nose as we wait our turn. Great-hearted animal, he is but a shadow of himself of two weeks back. We take care not to gripe our mounts as they greedily suck in the precious liquid.

We wait till our horses have taken the edge off their thirsts before drinking ourselves, then, as they become more restful, lower our heads and drink with them. I feel I could drink the well by myself but it is not wise to drink more than a few spoonfuls when one is water-starved as we are.

We feed the horses a little *tibbin* then turn to our own food. Some black bread and a quart of tea, neither sugar or milk. It is surprising how one can treat with almost epicurean pleasure food which ordinarily would be repulsive, when one's stomach has been maltreated as ours are.

Tired and weary we turn to the inevitable outposts. It is not difficult tonight to remain awake. The cries of the wounded out in no-man's land make sleep almost impossible.

We hear the shrieks of the wounded, piercing in their intensity, poor souls dying, lying in agony beyond help. They are between the two lines and beyond succour; to venture out there would restart the firing and bring the whole line into activity.

The fact that they are Turkish wounded does not harden our feelings, we would as willingly aid them as we would our own. It is doubtful if we have any hate for them, though we are opposed. They are like ourselves, puppets. It is the responsibility of the few that a nation fights, each side believing his cause is just and righteous.

The sun had risen a blood red this morning; bloody had been its course across the heavens and bloody its set. Many men, good and bad, have gone to their Maker this day.

Morning comes at last, a new day with its heat and flies and what else only God can tell. The sun perhaps has not the bloody glow of yesterday. Maybe the god of war has glutted his slavering maw enough for the nonce and wishes to digest the human sacrifice that has been offered him on the altar of greed.

Sacrifice it is, for any good that comes from war is a doubtful quantity. Those who fight are the givers; and those who make the wars and feed the fires, those who stay at home, they are the takers.

The wealthy man receives honour and position, for having his name associated with worthy objects, for allowing his organisations to be used in furtherance of the troops' comfort, for being at home, living at ease and safeguarding his own hide, for making equipment and supplying food and necessaries.

The lesser fellow shelters behind an excuse. He is perhaps not fit, or his conscience will not allow him to kill his fellow men. Which latter is a most laudable reason, but both are only a veil. It is lack of guts.

Those at home and who are not takers but givers, givers of their all, are the mothers and sisters and wives. Living in a world of insecurity, afraid to answer the postman's knock, theirs is sacrifice. There is no glory in war, only sorrow, suffering and illusion.

* * * * * * * *

As the day brightens we reset our saddles and file out, a dirty, lousy and unshaven crew. Forming into column we pass through what yesterday had been no-man's land and ride amongst the bodies, dead and dying, the aftermath of licensed murder.

Pitiable it is, and if the people of the world could but see it all, there would be no more wars.

Some are terribly maimed, perhaps have died instantly and not felt the torture which otherwise would have been theirs. Others lie still alive, suffering far more than we will ever know. Blackboy steps over *one* who feebly raises his hand, the only sign he is able to give that he still lives.

I know it is useless but step down and moisten his lips, then pour a little water into his parched mouth. He stares at me with eyes insane in their glitter. He will not live, perhaps it is better so, his suffering is not only killing his body, it has killed his brain.

He is but one, others there are who will never know who or what they have been. They will go through the tattered remnants of their shattered lives, gibbering idiots with minds twisted and torn, sheltering in a battered body. An offering for the world to see, a sacrifice to greed.

I can see another, and there are more like him, a chewed mass, an unfinished meal of that desert pariah, the desert dog. The fearsome death had been his which is so dreaded of the deserted wounded, the dog that preys on the dead and dying.

Everything is repulsive and revolting. I know in my mind that some of these are here because of me, I had helped to do this. Had done it at the command of a sheltered politician. There is no right in war, it is all wrong.

I feel sick at heart. I do not blame those who shirk at home. How can men with a right to live, to order their own lives, to act as they wish, be expected to offer themselves to such a fate?

The column moves on a little then stops as a block occurs. Little Jones climbs off his horse and spews his heart out. Spews with the revulsion of it all, a physical objection to war with its so-called glory.

He has not been with us long and is not so hardened. We do not look down on him for his weakness, some of us have done it before, would do it now perhaps, if we had a little more food in our bellies. As we move on, our ambulance comes up to do what it can. Some men are left behind to protect these defenceless bodies from the dogs and roving Bedouins, until they are moved away or graves dug. Graves for those who will for ever remain a mute protest against the damnable system that has put them there.

We do not envy those who are left as guardians; though they will be safe from shells and bullets, that is only their physical selves. The mental self will photograph this scene, it will be indelibly burned in their brains, they will carry this memory with them, always.

Such scenes sear the soul, leaving men apparently the same as their fellows but yet not the same. From the exterior we are all more or less the same, but within something gets twisted and is torn so that joys are deadened and laughter does not come so easily.

We may be young in years but old in sorrow. A generation of youth is being lost in these dread years. The generation, or what will be left of it, will continue to live, but their minds will be far ahead of their years, so that physically there will be a generation, or part of it, but mentally there will not. The world will be too busy to halt and reason this out, so that those who cannot keep up will just drop out, lost. When the need is gone a grateful country will soon forget; it is human nature.

****

Everything seems comparatively quiet and still. We have been in every action so far and are tired and worn. Our horses cannot move at more than a canter. Lack of hard food, grain and the long thirsts are telling on them. If we are to remain a useful unit a rest is necessary. We have not reasoned this out; that the main body have forged ahead of us indicates this.

I can hear firing a long way off. We are not amongst it so I do not care.

We are riding in a field overgrown with wild thyme. Its odour strongly assails my nostrils. I think of roast dinners I have had; I can imagine the seasoning. Foolish to think this way, it only increases hunger.

I have no tobacco, so roll myself a cigarette made of tea. One does not feel hunger so much when smoking.

We ride along at ease, no troubling thoughts of a coming charge. My mind revolves back through the past weeks, weeks of sorrows and joys. The sorrows are known, the joys lay in the friendships that form under these sifting conditions, when a man's good and bad are open for all to see.

We learn to value our friends, to know what they mean to us. We each depend on the other, if one is weak we all fall. Friendships made this way are forged and tested in the white-hot heat of the great divide. We know more of each other than would ever be known under any other circumstances; we learn to love and appreciate our friendships accordingly.

CHAPTER 2

The Raid

Weeks have gone past and still the campaign drags on. We are miles north of our setting-out point. The country is constantly changing. From the desert sands with their roaming Bedouins we are entering the firmer ground of Palestine. We have encountered a few Jewish settlements and seen patches of cultivation. The milk and honey of the Bible are still missing, but the wilderness at least is becoming less and less.

Coming to an Arab village with a plentiful water supply we halt for a day to rest the horses. We have not had a wash or shaved our beards for something like three weeks. I am losing track of the days.

Last night my feet had been aching damnably. The sweat has run into my boots for weeks and stayed there, they have never been off. The flesh must be showing signs of the rot we get.

Riding along in the darkness, half-crazy for sleep, I had been thinking in a delirious sort of way about my feet. I had wondered how they would look when eventually I did get my boots off.

By their feel I knew my socks fitted solidly, had almost become part of them. The stink is no longer noticeable, we have long since grown used to the smell of sweaty feet; it is only when the air is tainted with a different sort of smell that we notice anything. I had been riding along, thinking how they would look when finally I got my feet separated from my socks. Would the sock pattern be worked in dirt on them so that it would seem I still wore them? Perhaps they would stand up of their own accord. Then I wondered how the socks would wash. Would they be hard and brittle and break, or would they be so impregnated with dirt that washing would dissolve them?

Thinking only made them ache the more. It is so long since my boots have been off that perhaps my socks have rotted away. I could feel the foot-rot by moving my toes.

It is not only my boots that have not been off; my clothes too have not been removed, not even my leggings. To be able to wash now will be pleasant indeed. To get my trousers off and kill the troublesome lice that keep biting, and bathe my behind which is all red and chafed through too much riding on a sweaty seat.

Brent minds the horses whilst we three go for water. We take our canvas buckets and water bottles. I get my razor and shave the itching hair off my face, then wet my body and rub it carefully with a little piece of soap I have. We pour the water over each other to wash the lather off. How good it feels! It makes one fresh and the perpetual tiredness seems to drop off like a cloak. My bowels are heavy, I search for a likely place to empty them. I have piles from excessive riding, the seat of my trousers is stained red. Banks jokes about this till I look at his and find the same.

I attend to Blackboy's back, it has galled a little. For some days I have been leading him and riding one of the spares whose rider has passed on.

The day passes all too quickly. The short rest only serves to makes us feel our weariness the more. We sleep at peace this night and move on again tomorrow morning.

* * * * * * * *

We ride along the bottom of a stony *wadi* bed. The little dust we make serves as an indicator to a Turkish battery whose whole attention seems to be centred in our little sphere.

They are falling uncomfortably close, too close for Blunt, whose cowardly soul is reflected on his white face. He always was a shirker and a nuisance in our troop. He would drink his water long before we had made an impression on ours and then beg most abjectly for a drink. It is an unwritten law not to ask another for water when this precious substance is scarce.

It is common for men to duck their heads when the shells are low, one does it instinctively. With Blunt it is yellowness, he ducks when others do not move, when others duck, he almost prays.

The explosions are so close that we fear a hit each minute. Sayer keeps calling to Blunt that he can hear the shells whistling his number. When a shell comes near, Sayer repeats Blunt's number so as to imitate its whine.

This makes him more nervous till he becomes crazed with fear. He is riding in silence, possibly afraid to speak. As I watch him he splits the air with a release of gastric gases, does it unconsciously. Fear does do that sometimes. We tell him to ride alone. He is afraid to move away, our closeness makes him feel safer. As he persists in remaining in the troop, we ride apart from him.

I forget about Blunt as I feel Blackboy cast a shoe; that is two now, it would be foolish to ride him farther. I ask the farrier to put them on again. He does not like stopping in this unfriendly country. I persuade him and we draw aside and let the column pass.

The afternoon is drawing on when the task is finished. The troop have disappeared from sight. We ride on in the dark, trusting more to instinct and sense of direction than to definite knowledge of our course, till we meet some of the Inverness battery who give us correct bearings.

* * * * * * * *

Coming near to the coast we halt for two days. Our lead horses are to be sent back to the remounts following in our rear; I am detailed to do this and so lose the spell the others will have.

I return on the second evening and find the regiment has gone: they were not to have left till tomorrow morning.

I follow blindly on in the direction I expect them to take. For hours I do not see any life. Later I meet detached units but they cannot guide me.

Thirst has been tormenting me for hours and Blackboy too. Constantly we have searched for signs of water, followed along dry *wadi* beds hoping against hope to find water, if only a puddle. Topping a rise we see a trickle near to which a body of Yeomanry are encamped, possibly delayed for a day's rest.

31

Cantering forward I fling myself from the saddle, remove Blackboy's bit, and heads side by side, we slake our burning thirsts in the muddied water.

As I rise erect preparatory to filling my bottles an irate officer gallops up and asks if I am quite devoid of intelligence. In answer to the look of enquiry I gave him he pointed to a board a little farther up the bed on which had been rudely scrawled *Bilharzia Beware!* and then to a second which read *Chlorinated Water.*

I had been too thirsty to think of such a possibility as the water being contaminated with the dread Bilharzia, but if such was the case it was too late now, my belly was full of it. Still I have drunk infected water before, water with the hook worm in it, and so far have not been troubled. It is a risk we constantly take, so much of the scattered water about Palestine's plains is diseased in some form, and nearly always what we drink has been chlorinated first. I have had belly pains on more than one occasion from bad water, had dysentery too; who hasn't? Shortage of water and diseased water are but two of the unavoidable hardships we have long since grown used to.

Unable to secure any definite directions from the officer, now quite friendly, I walked over to the chlorinated tank, filled my bottles and mounting Blackboy rode on.

Towards nightfall I meet a battalion of Lowland Scottish moving from one side of the line to the other. Knowing they will stop soon I decide to follow and sleep with them.

We have always admired these little men. It is as one sees them now, making a forced march, that their qualities are appreciated. Through the blistering heat of the day they have marched without thought of giving in.

The great heavy pack of the infantryman which envelopes and weighs him down, becomes a terrible burden when the sun is high. They march along, the sweat pouring down their faces, soaking their clothes, running into their eyes and half blinding them. The dust they stir swirls about them, then settles on their faces, turning to mud.

Great iron-shod boots torturing their feet; each hour making them grow heavier as their feet weary, their feet sorer as the sweat pouring down their legs fills their boots. The pack straps rub their backs till they grow red and raw, but still onward they go. Some lag behind, falter and drop, stagger to their feet and struggle on. Jotted through the column I can see men supported by their comrades, their legs moving automatically. With bodies numbed, their legs are driven by that indomitable spirit which drives them on, constantly on.

Their pluck is astounding. Bred for the most part in cities, to a measure brought up in squalor, in mean streets with little opportunity to develop physically. Driven early to work, mostly in shops, or to pore over books in offices and grow weedy. Knowing little of any town but that in which they had their being. Their lives sedentary, with nothing to prepare them for the hardships of war. From this material come these wonderful little men. If they have not the physique, they have the will and the spirit.

Riding up to the end of the column I am greeted with a smile, a cheery word. I notice some of the weaker, who have gradually worked through the column, coming to the end they struggle along blindly. Knowing they will have their hourly spells, they keep on, waiting to catch up.

I dismount and place one on my saddle, and give two others a stirrup-leather each. The one riding sways about, unused to a saddle. Blackboy pricks up his ears, in objection to this unskilled burden, perhaps wondering if he should throw him. My hand on the bridle rein, close up, keeps him quiet.

It is not long and darkness sets in. They cannot guide me but I decide to stay the night here. They sit about and make me welcome. I listen to their talk and learn something of their lives.

I see some of their backs, rubbed red and raw. The khaki drill tunics they wear do not absorb the sweat, they only become sodden and irritate.

* * * * * * * *

The regiment is switching across the line. We halt for an hour to rest. Brent holds the horses whilst we search for something to boil our quart-pots. The ground is patched here and there with a sort of half-dead grass.

We scrape this up with our fingers, painfully and slowly, groping in the dark. It takes a long time, we have to gather almost a blade at a time. Placing the four quart pots in a circle we light the grass in the middle. As it burns we keep adding a little more grass, very carefully. We are unable to gather sufficient to boil the water. When it is a little more than warm we add the tea and are content with this half-stewed mixture. The black tea—we have neither sugar or milk—with some bully and broken biscuits provides our meal. We are not fully fed, no soldier ever was.

Near midnight we move on and ride till daylight. Shortly after sunrise we come under shell fire; it is light and we are able to ride out of it.

A Jewish village is just ahead, we ride towards it spying out the land. Our batteries are not far behind, ready to fire if the Turks should open.

As we enter the only street of the village four shells come over in quick succession. One explodes very near me, a flying splinter hitting the cantle of my saddle as I sit at ease. Instinctively I move Blackboy a few paces away, then feel foolish. I may just as likely move towards an oncoming shell as away from it.

Gaining little information at this village, we ride on to an Arab settlement some two miles away. Within half a mile of it, the troop shelters behind a knoll whilst Winn and I ride ahead, they covering us.

We go forward like a piece of bait, a decoy. If we emerge safely we can tell the troop leader what the position is. If we don't, there will be no need to, he will know.

It is not very comfortable this riding in advance. We feel a little like Blunt did back in the *wadi* bed.

We find nothing unusual at this village. A few dirty Arabs cowering out of sight and the usual goats and fowls. It is only the riskiness of our mission that saves those fowls. Still we may later return, they are bony and ancient but for all that food.

We wait by the village till the troop canters up. Our officer considers awhile, mentally reviewing the position. Turning to Winn and me, he tells us to continue on to the next settlement. I have time to whisper to Smith about the fowls, if it is humanly possible he will get some of them.

The settlement ahead is Jewish and far larger than the one we are leaving and also more isolated. The likelihood of drawing fire here is greatly increased. It is little comfort that should the enemy decide to take the bait, we will be avenged. We much prefer that the bait is left alone.

As we near the village I can feel my heart thumping. A single shot passes wide away, a sniper. He fires another, a little closer this time. The Turkish rifleman is very accurate at a distance. Evidently they will not use artillery, knowing full well it is what we want them to do, so we can turn our batteries on them.

Turning to Winn, I ask him if he thinks we will make it. I can see by the look on his face that he is a little doubtful. I feel like galloping these last couple of hundred yards, but then that may spoil everything.

It seems to take us hours to cover these last few yards, it is only minutes. The sniper is still keeping at us, I am thinking and I know Winn's thoughts are parallel to mine, of what lies behind those mud walls.

The horses seem to feel the tenseness that possesses us, they urge to trot these last few yards. I hold Blackboy back and we walk steadily through the outer line of mud walls.

We ride amongst the houses, relaxed like a sprinter who has made a finishing burst of speed. The inhabitants stand in doorways and watch us. They do not know our intention and seem quite harmless.

We search around but find no signs of Turkish occupation. Winn rides to the. wall through which we had entered and signals the troop to come up. Whilst he is doing this I enter one of the houses and find some cognac.

I offer money for it but the man is averse to taking it, he has had experience of Turkish notes and thinks Egyptian are bad too. I intend to have that cognac, as he will not sell it that is his loss and my saving. Reaching out I grasp two bottles. He breaks into voluble Hebrew and tries to get them back. It is too late now, I push him away towards a chair, he stumbles and falls over it. When he has recovered I am in the street. It is safer there.

Winn rides up and we open a bottle. It is fire-water and as we have not had any liquor for months we decide to wait till we are with the main body before drinking it. Anything may happen here; we do not wish to risk being drunk on doubtful liquor in country like this.

The troop look around and finding nothing of importance, ride back towards the Jewish village. We have not gone far when it is discovered that Blunt is missing. Returning to the village we search but can find no trace of him. It is getting dark, we cannot afford to linger here.

* * * * * * * *

We spend two days near the Jewish village, patrolling the area till supplies come up and we are able to forge on again.

Some distance away is an Arab village that we have not been in. A patrol is sent across to it. Smith asks that he may go with it. He says there may be some Arab women there, less ugly than those we have been seeing. He says he has a burning in his vitals that only female association can subdue. Whether they will be complacent or not does not seem to occur to him.

It is late afternoon, we are waiting for darkness to cover our movements as we swing into another sector of the line. A patrol comes in leading a figure dressed in the conventional Jewish garb. A round black hat like a parson wears and a long black coat. It is Blunt, returning like a bad penny that cannot be lost.

We go over to the patrol to see this wandering Jew. The patrol do not know him and have brought him here for identification. Somebody says it would be a good joke to feign ignorance as to who he is.

We walk across as Blunt comes near, his face showing confidence now that he is amongst fellows he knows. He asks Smith to tell the patrol he belongs to this troop. Smith shakes his head and says he doesn't know him, he certainly isn't Blunt, the fellow he claims to be, that Blunt has been killed. He turns to us and we confirm his remark.

The patrol seem doubtful as to what they should do till Blunt says that Headquarters will know him. They take him there. We would like to go and see what happens but too much curiosity may bring the Colonel's wrath down on us. We at least have the excuse that his Wandering Jew disguise misled us.

The Colonel wastes little time. He sends for the troop officer, who recognises him. This point determined he sends him back to the troop till the stunt is over. He will then be court-martialled for desertion.

He tells us that we left him behind and as a Turkish patrol was coming up, he had to hide in a *wadi* bed. He managed to steal the Jewish garb and has been living in constant fear, trying to make his way back to our lines, his black clothes hiding his too obvious uniform. We know that it was the cognac. He found some and wishing to keep it to himself had brought this on his head through his greed.

It is just getting dark as we ride out. We keep moving all night, working across towards the coast from the foothills. We have a short spell at daybreak then continue on again.

Near midday we come to a small flat plain that has seen a nasty battle a few days previously. A number of Turkish and a few British dead are lying about, food for the flies. Some effort has been made to bury them, but the few graves that have been dug are far too shallow; the jackals have been at them.

A few days of sun and a few nights of jackals have left a sickening sight, but one to which we are not strangers. Some men and some horses are lying on their sides, with bellies swollen and their entrails protruding. It is bad enough that this should happen to horses, but worse that human flesh should end this way. Even if they were Turks, that does not alter the fact that they are flesh and blood, human beings as we are; the only difference is that they are the enemy. Mothers have suffered to bring these men into this world, have watched them grow into manhood, only to see them snatched away to fight the battles of nations. They would be told they had been killed in action. All to end like this; a corpse left lying to feed the jackals.

Some vultures are wheeling overhead, waiting for us to pass; we have disturbed their meal. The air is strong with the stink of rotting flesh, blue faces stare up at us, some with the eyes missing.

I look at the scene and wonder as others wonder, if we too may end this way. Would we too some day lie out in a plain, without a grave? Perhaps have a cross set up over a few bones? Where here is the glory in dying for one's country, what glory is there that men should end thus?

* * * * * * * *

All day we have fought a running battle. As we drove the Turk from one position he fled to yet another. We followed but never quite caught him. We have not eaten all day, in fact not since yesterday. Our tongues are lolling in our mouths, withered sticks. We can hardly speak, our lips are hard and dry, our eyes enlarged and red.

The sweat pouring down our faces has mingled with the dust, turning to mud, some of it entering our eyes. Night is falling and still we have not caught up. It seems the Turk will escape us after all. As we follow in his wake we pass many dead and wounded, dropped by the way. The horses are giving out, their breathing is heavy and laboured, their bellies red, eyes staring. We cannot ask them to go much farther.

We drag ourselves to still one more hill, dismount and man the ridge. Our little Hotchkiss buzzes into life at the end of the troop line, but its noise is quickly drowned by the roar of our beloved Ayrshire battery behind us. So close that we almost imagine we feel the hot breath of the gun barrels as they spew their shrieking shells low down overhead. The Turk is using light artillery, but he too is feeling the strain, his aim is growing faulty. He seems to think that darkness is his only hope, his lack of precision is more than compensated by his greater determination. The light gradually fails and leaves us in possession of our knoll and the Turk of his. The position is fraught with anxiety and delicate in the extreme. The Turk, though on the run, is infinitely superior to us in numbers. Should he turn in the night and attack, anything may happen. The horses are left some hundreds of yards to the rear; every available man is on the ridge.

The night passes slowly. The only sounds, an occasional machine-gun burst or isolated rifle fire. As morning draws near we stand to and wait. The sun rises, blossoming into light diffusing the country in its early morning glow. As the day grows it becomes apparent why the night was so unexpectedly quiet. The Turk, under cover of darkness has retired across a small depression to a farther ridge, where signs of feverish activity are visible. It seems he is digging-in prior to a more determined attempt to stem our advance.

For weeks we have steadily pushed the enemy back and back, knowing a stop must eventually come to his retreat, but not expecting it here. The farther we advance, the nearer to his base and source of supplies comes the Turk, and we are correspondingly farther away. Our supply-columns following in the rear cannot cope with the gigantic task of feeding such an army of men and horses, even though to a great extent we live on the country.

We move forward to the position vacated by the Turk. Both sides now occupy eminences overlooking the same intervening depression; to advance across which in daylight would be annihilation. A small party is sent to scour for water and we remain for digging. We are too weakened by privation and too low in strength to attack a trench system such as is appearing ahead. The few hours rest we have snatched during the night have only served to let our tiredness obtain a greater grip on us. Our bones ache and our joints are stiff, whilst the need of water is making us frantic.

All day we toil and sweat under the boiling sun. Dig, dig, dig for hours with a few minutes' spell at intervals. Every now and again we become careless and make targets of ourselves to draw enemy fire. He does the same too, so that those who rest have to exchange the rifle for the pick.

Late in the afternoon a regiment of horse come up and take over our left flank, whilst a battalion of Camels come into the right. They too commence this feverish digging, which all keep up right through the night. A raiding party go out shortly after dark covered by our artillery. Whilst the barrage is on we rest. It is not safe above ground, our guns are firing from only a few hundred yards in our rear and their shells falling almost in front, howitzer fashion. As it is some fall amongst us, the gunners' accuracy lost by the shortness of the range.

With daylight we are able to survey our position and see the shape our night digging has made of the position. We have a rough circle of trenches, redoubt-fashion, with a sap running to each flank. These saps are extremely difficult to dig. Their course led us through loose sand which fell back as fast as we dug it out. Sometimes we would be down about six feet when the sides would come tumbling in, burying whoever was unlucky enough to be working there. We would leave our trench-digging and turn to rescuing the buried. They would come out with the sand sticking to their sweat-soaked clothes, in their eyes and nose, spitting it from their mouths.

Towards afternoon the digging ceases. Our gun is given a position of advantage in the front trench which overlooks the flat in front. I draw the first observation shift and amuse myself potting at odd Turks who keep bobbing up ahead. Others lay behind at rest, or on other posts. Some are playing cards in the funk holes we have dug behind the main entrenchment. A shell comes over and falls right behind, I drop out of sight till it explodes then resume my sniping till another sends me flying to shelter.

I think we have all become fatalists long ago. It is difficult to think otherwise. The miraculous escapes of some, and the extreme bad luck of others, lead one to thinking these things must be decided and are not just matters of chance. Four fellows in the supports had found their funk hole too windy for cards and moved to another. They had barely vacated the first hole when a direct hit from a Turkish shell blew it to pieces. They escaped by seconds.

I saw a sergeant having his hair clipped in a back position, considered absolutely safe. A spent bullet caught his shoulder and penetrated to his chest. He died within the hour. It was only a bullet on the drop could have fallen into the place where he was.

This morning, whilst back with the horses, I had been sitting with my back against a small cliff. For half an hour I had been there and not one shell came over. An officer rode past, I had idly watched him as he passed across my view. A shell whined down and hit the horse he was riding in the behind, exploding internally. It blew the officer some yards away. He got up unhurt except for bruises and fragments of his horse plastered about him. In half an hour this was the only shell to come over. It makes us wonder, these things do not just come about, some influence seems always to be present, some unknown thing which we call fate.

* * * * * * * *

We lie waiting to go over; each night a raid is made. Those who are detailed for it know hours ahead, which produces a nervous tension difficult to bear. It will be preluded by a five-minutes barrage. When our guns cease, the Turkish will take up the hymn, through which we will advance. It does not seem possible that men can go through the hail of iron which falls from overhead, but somehow they go out and somehow they come back. The hundreds of craters make it more difficult to understand. We are never very clear about it all.

Our nerves become keyed to breaking-point, and we seem to run as if driven by some power over which we have no control. I do not think we are ever quite sane when we make these raids. No man could lie calmly on his belly whilst the earth heaves under him, then jump up and run through fire and death, waiting for death, dealing out death whilst he waited.

As I lie I can hear the staccato bark of the machine-guns. The clock slowly creeps around, ever so slowly and yet quickly, Slowly because of the tension and quickly because these may be our last minutes on earth. For many it will be, but who these are we do not know. As the clock reaches five minutes to eight, overhead goes a whistling and whining, followed immediately by a double roar, one the discharging guns, the other the detonating shells. All becomes a bedlam of sound, we cannot distinguish between the guns and the shells. The sighing overhead is drowned, the earth heaves and shakes under us, the night is lit by explosions. We lie and shiver and shake; we are not cold, we are impervious to bodily sensation, our minds think only of one thing. The devil dwells on earth and for a little while this will be his particular hell. We lie crouched, ready, rifles loaded and bayonets fixed, grenades handy.

A hand seems to hold my heart, to squeeze it, my breath is irregular, a band is around my head. I do not have to speak, if I did I could not. I fear, am afraid; of what? It is not death, I do not fear that, for death is oblivion, I do not know just what it is. I shake and move my head, it is impossible to keep still, my limbs move involuntarily. I want to swallow but cannot, I feel I am choking. The minutes are creeping by, creeping ever so slowly. How long just five little minutes take to pass! The shelling stops, a second of silence and the Turkish guns commence to drone. In this second of silence we rise and move forward, each man with a mission, every man with the same mission, to kill.

We rush down the sloping hillside out into the flat. Men are falling already, some had hardly risen from the ground before fate overtook them. My mind is chaotic. I rush madly on, shells flash and roar but still I go on. I see others fall but nothing impedes or stops me in this mad rush. I am still afraid; but in a nebulous way I seem now to know what it is I fear. It is not death, my fear is all around me. I see men lose their limbs, torn off as if an invisible hand had removed them. They fall to the ground, mutilated, shrieking as they drop. I see a man bend back from the middle like a hinge and collapse, a misshapen bundle, almost halved by a machine-gun burst. That is what I fear, I know now; to be blind or have no legs or arms, mutilation, pain and agony. I know this night will leave many such, with life in their bodies but death in their souls. Their bodies but a shell to carry the remnant of their former selves.

42

A bump in the ground rises up in front. We crouch behind it waiting for the stragglers to come up. My mind runs riot, a swirling and seething is in my brain, my thoughts are disjointed and unconnected. My head seems as if it must burst. I curse the bloody war and those who made it, curse the God that permits it and Christ who died for us as we die now, for what? Must one's very soul be torn to shreds? Will that barrage never, never stop? I shrink into myself, cringing and cringing and yet feeling that I grow larger, become an increasingly greater target. I expect each minute to be the last, I must get hit, how can I help it, luck is lasting too long. A five-nine explodes behind, too close, the next may be it, I hear it coming. The shelling dies, oh God, end it and let me be at rest! I hear them calling, ready to charge; would that I had the courage to run away, but no! I must go on.

Another barrage comes down, we charge on and pass through. The bayonet was ever a cursed thing, he will stick it through my belly. He comes at me, I lunge I know not how, it gets him and he falls. I cannot free the blade, it sticks. I have never used the bayonet before. We used to be told to fire a cartridge to loosen it when it jammed, it must be stuck in bone. Heave and it comes away, to leave a gibbering mass that once was a man. I rush forward to stumble and fall and lie gasping. The shells lessen, will they start again?

Like a curtain that is raised, my brain clears. I no longer fear, the grip on my heart slackens. I know what I am doing, have control over my actions, I move and act without the madness that has controlled me. I know what is happening about me, can see and understand, the mental mist which has obscured everything is clearing away. The shelling gradually dies down, machine-guns still rack the night but gone is that maddening rush of men, killing, killing, killing.

Groping my way back, half walking, half crawling, scrambling along as best I can, I hear a cry, I stop and listen, at first I cannot place it though it is very near. I crawl to where I think it is only to hear it in another direction. I crawl this way and still do not locate it. I lie still and listen, slowly and hesitatingly I move to where I am sure it comes from. Edging over the top of a small rise I hear it issuing from a crevice beneath. Crawling down I see a form, writhing and moaning in agony. Turning it over I find he is one of ours and but a boy. He is badly shot through the stomach and is very far gone. Belly wounds often are fatal even when taken to hospital, the sepsis penetrates.

He holds his hand against the wound, whether to stop the blood which is slowly oozing through his fingers, or to ease the pain, I do not know. The only good it does is to hold him together, the stomach flesh is gone. The pity of it all, the infinite pity. A boy who should still be at home, he has tried, and in trying has died, for dead he will be very soon. I put my arm around him and support his head. His mind is far away, he does not realise that someone holds him. He asks for water, I haven't any, no need for any on a raid. I try to soothe him but the wound has turned his head.

I feel nauseated and sick at heart. The stark shattering realism of everything that war stands for has penetrated me tonight as never before. I have stood in the dark valley as many, many others have, have looked death in the face, have felt its clammy hand reaching out to me. I have known fear, deep terrifying fear, fear of the crashing annihilation which has swirled around and swept us along like flotsam, bits of human life, legitimate prey of the Martian god, offered as a sacrifice to greed, the greed of nations, the greed of power, the greed for wealth. The agony and pain, the wanton destruction of youthful manhood with its aftermath of misery and suffering, has seared into my very soul. What a mockery it all is, what a mockery that phrase they were always preaching to us: 'For God, King and Country.' The King has naught to do with it—why link his name with such a hypocritical sham? It should be 'For the Devil, Hell and Greed.' If there is still a God, why does He permit such as this when the talisman of His preaching is 'Love Thy Fellow Men'?

We will shortly go back for a spell and the padre will call a church parade and say, 'Our Father which art in Heaven,' better that he said 'The Devil who dwells in Hell and we his disciples.'

When the war is finished, the ministers will wonder why the churches are empty. Who can feel the fervour of a faith which preaches peace to all men who on earth do dwell, then drops its tenets by the wayside and encourages slaughter and desolation to a fair country and the divine creation which peoples it? Perhaps the exponents of the Bible can tell, but to me it is beyond understanding. The war is dealing to religion a blow from which it will never recover. To lend a war the sanctified blessing of an inconsistent church is but blasphemy cloaked by a phrase, 'For God and Country.'

By pain we come into the world, and in pain they who pass on through war's bloody maw go out. It is all about me now, I can hear groans and cries. A convulsive movement in my arms, a sighing sob and another broken life is gathered in to prove, or disprove, the verity of our faith.

I struggle up and continue back. I see and hear the dead and dying, hear their shrieks and agonised calls. I feel the hopeless drift of it all, the useless-ness of this slaughter, for when it is all over no one will have gained, we will all have lost. A few will have more wealth, more power, that is all. The mass gains nothing and loses much.

As I fall into a trench an officer passes by. He stops to speak, then changes his mind and goes on. Perhaps there is a glitter in my eyes, a mad look. I do not feel sane, something had been twisted and torn within me. He has been through it all before, he knows, so he says nothing. Tomorrow it will be all right, yes tomorrow it will be all right. Tomorrow the shock will have passed, but the tomorrow will never come which can erase such memories. The friends of today are a memory of tomorrow; next week others will be a memory, for many a sad one. Nights such as these can never be effaced from the minds of those who have known them.

* * * * * * * *

It is raining, the first signs of the wet season. We shiver with the cold we are not used to. The hot breath of the desert has inured us to heat, has thinned our blood. This sudden change chills us to the bone. We have no shelters and stand about like drowned rats, for the heavens have literally opened and let the water fall in a solid mass.

We have handed our redoubt over to the infantry. Our farewells to it are tinged with sorrow and regrets, but we are wearily glad to see an end of it.

As for me, I feel an imbued bitterness that hitherto has not penetrated, despite many weary months of campaigning. Now after just a few days I feel entirely changed, filled with a spirit of sad rebellion, whereas I had hitherto accepted everything as it came, it was the war, what could one? I had my faiths, and beliefs, these helped me along; but now, I can no longer lean to my creed, I feel it is a sham. An unutterable loneliness, a desperate-ness seems to envelope me. Perhaps it will pass away, recent happenings are too vividly fresh in my mind. To go through life with fixed and asserted principles and beliefs teaches one to lean to them for support. To find a doubt of them, a suggestion that the solace they should offer is a mockery, that the faith they profess is an hypocrisy, makes me very bitter, bitter with a bitterness that I cannot shake off.

It is coming night, we have no shelter from the rain. I dig myself a V shaped trench on a hillside and lie on the sodden earth within its arms which help to run the water away. I stretch my waterproof sheet over me and run my hand through Blackboy's bridle and place it in my pocket. Thus secured I try to sleep, lulled by the down-coming torrents.

CHAPTER 3

Rum, Whisky, Wine & Bad Women

The blue Mediterranean stretches away below me to a limitless horizon, nearby at the foot of the hill on which I stand I can see the waves curl and break, the foam scintillating in reflection of the sun's rays. I feel happier than I have for weeks; something in the gloriousness of nature around me, so different from the dun brown monotony of past weeks, makes the world brighter; it is not such a bad place. A little sadness lingers in my mind, memories of lost friends and a delusion. The stunt has given its last convulsive kick; in a few days we move back to a convenient railhead to rest.

Banks will be along in a few minutes, then we will both take a look at the town (Jaffa), the first we have encountered during the campaign. Coming over a rise the first view we had of it suggested visions of deflective relaxation we are anxious to taste. The orange groves are prolific and are now a mass of golden fruit; our lips still smart from the rind of the dozens we have eaten. Everyone is keen with anticipation, for surely here a soldier's three wants, wine, women, and tobacco, can be appeased.

Seeing Banks in the distance I hurry after him, and we walk into the town together. Coming along the main street we encounter a café, its sign still wet with the paint which has given it a new name, written in straggling English with the Union Jack in the background. Instinctively we turn our steps towards the door, our thoughts only of food and to be able to fill our bellies to repletion. It is a dirty place inside (and so is the food) but we care little about that.

I do not know what we are eating, probably goat; there is plenty of it, which is all that matters. We wash it down with sour wine, in preference to tea without milk and sweetened with honey. The wine is not very good either, but after the first two bottles we do not notice this and call for a third. A full stomach seasoned with plenty of wine soon robs us of care, so we sally forth to see what we can and find what enjoyment there is.

Along the outer edge of the town Banks draws my attention to some khaki-clad figures outside a house; a second hovel a few yards farther along also has its little group. Curiosity leads us towards them, though we should have known what they portended. If women are to be found, there is always a type who will do so; it is probably the reaction that sends them seeking such society. A soldier has an instinctive sense for feminine companionship, seems to want for its softening influence after days and weeks of stark realities. Banks looked the scene over, but showed no desire to join; he probably does not feel any mental disturbance by its suggestion. I can see one of the women now, a type who could so easily plunge one into the hell her appearance typifies; undoubtedly diseased. I am thankful the urge is not strong within me and that I am able to pass by; women like this will keep it so; they are not the type who in later life I would care to mingle in my thoughts. Of a kind common enough, preying on the half-intoxicated or those who have passed the stage of caring, and unable to realise the significance of their suggestion. Women who under ordinary circumstances would be avoided.

It does not take us long to exhaust the town. We gather in some more of their cheap wine and wander back to the lines in time to water the horses. This done, we waste little time before crawling into our blankets; the night looks like being chilly and we are very tired.

Another day comes, we water our horses again, and then begins the long trek back to the railhead. The first night we ride till dark before stopping to rest. I dismount and unsaddle where I stand; it is very dark so that I have to feel the ground for somewhere to lie. My hand encounters a slight rise that forms a natural pillow. The air seems a little tainted, but I am too weary to worry about that. With the coming of morning I find the source of the smell I had noticed last night. My pillow is a hastily dug grave, and bits of the half-buried body stick through the mound. The jackals have been at it in their usual way. The first thing I see on waking is a piece of rotting thigh-bone.

Another day's riding brings us to the edge of the sand dunes, which run towards the coast some four miles away. With the rainy season coming on, the sand will make an excellent camp. This week is the first time I have seen rain for a year.

How glorious it is to laze here! We have little to do but necessary camp fatigues, groom and feed the horses, and draw rations and forage from railhead. The horse lines are cleaned daily and the usual camp sanitation is attended to. This latter is simple, just a long trench with a bar along the top. In addition to this we have long lengths of galvanised piping, tapering from eight inches or so at the top to two at the base. These are sunk into the ground to half their length in groups, usually of three. When the ground becomes saturated we simply move the pipes to a new spot, and when the camp is ended they go into the baggage train. We have no privacy in these necessary operations, but none is needed, we have long since overcome our natural modesty. Amongst ourselves it does not matter and there are few locals to see. If Arab women wander along at awkward moments it is regrettable, but unavoidable; but the type who frequents the camps would scarcely be troubled by such matters.

Some clippers have arrived so that we can cut the long hair of our horses. Blackboy has a rooted objection to being handled by anyone but myself; he is spirited and dislikes the buzzing of the turning handle. Cajole him as I may, it is useless; we end by throwing him and running the clippers over him as he lies on the sand struggling, snorting and kicking. He is full of ticks too. Each morning I spend half an hour going over his belly removing them. They are big fellows, and when fully inflated become as large as the blowflies which pester us. Every morning I remove dozens of these pestilent little animals, only to find more the next day. They congregate only on his belly, and they congregate without end. We also clip our own heads; our hair is long and hot and it is a relief to have it short to the scalp.

Some days we drill in gas-helmets. We have not yet received the new type. The kind we have are made of flannel, sack shape, and fit over our heads. We button them in our tunics and breathe through a mouthpiece attachment. The flannel is saturated with chemicals which pollute our mouths for hours. Gas has proved very disastrous in Palestine: one never knows which way it will blow. Often it returns, with dire results, to those who emitted it, which is something to be thankful for: and the air too is so hot that very often it rises and passes over.

* * * * * * * *

Christmas has come at last. We have been expecting a lot from this usually festive season as we are spelling. But we reckoned without the rains, which have washed away miles of railway, and incidentally the train bringing our Christmas mail and parcels from home. The few packages that are recovered are mostly ruined with water. However, there are still the comfort clubs and societies which professedly work for the good of the soldier.

A Horse Racing Club is very good to us, sending sufficient of the things which appeal to us, canned fruits and such like, to provide one really decent meal all round. We are truly grateful and thank them from the bottom of our hearts. The Y.M.C.A. which works for the common soldiers' good also remembered us, in a fashion. Each man received a box from this all-generous institution. The boxes are all the same, except that some have tobacco and others cigarettes. Mine is composed of a tin of milk and coffee mixed, two small packets of cigarettes, a tooth-brush and powder, and a pair of bootlaces. The irony of it all! We take our packages, rush to open them, and find—what? Bootlaces! The only thing edible—a tin of milk and coffee. We thank the powers that tonight there is a rum issue.

Our rum issue is more than acceptable, but it has two drawbacks. Firstly the quantity, each man receiving one tot which from our point of view is too meagre. Sometimes but not often we supplement it by obtaining the issue of someone else who does not want it. The second complaint is quality. Doubtless it is good rum when originally obtained but the quality sadly deteriorates before reaching us. We suspect that the various channels it passes through result in adulteration. The Supply Service would take a little and add water to make the measure. So on it would go, till finally it was too weak to water any more. By the taste it often seems as if the quantity is then made up of methylated spirits, or for that matter of anything handy. We generally allude to it as furniture polish.

Smith is in trouble today. Last night he was on guard duty over a ration dump. During a night shift he broached a demi of rum and drank more than he should; he started singing; so now he is resting in the guard tent. I went down to see him after stables this morning. He was still partially drunk, and sufficiently happy to be unconcerned about his probable punishment.

A new medical officer joined the regiment a few days ago. We saw him out riding this afternoon for the first time. I don't think he has ever been on a horse before, for he kept sliding along the saddle like a novice, one hand holding the horse's mane. We *barracked* him from behind a sand dune, but so far nothing has been done about that. Lenny goes each day to the medical tent for dressings, he says he seems a regular fellow. He swears a lot, Lenny says, which would hall mark him in his opinion. He cannot be any worse than the last one we had.

* * * * * * * *

We are moving our camp a day's ride nearer the line, and the railway is being pushed on so that we will still be close for supplies. It has been raining for days but fortunately today, when we move, is fine.

The head of the column is entering a muddy lagoon formed by the recent rains, with water a little more than fetlock deep. Stuck in the middle is a Holt tractor, waiting for the mud to dry up. Someone is riding across to it; his horse does not like the tractor, and is prancing a little. The foolish rider pulls the bridle-rein too much; he has the horse on its hind legs, pivoting about like a dancer. He has pulled the rein too much, and now both of them are floundering in the mud. The rider looks very doleful, standing there with the slush running off him, while his horse is careering away, and he doesn't know what to do about it.

We pass odd graves scattered here and there. They are mostly shallow—dug in a hurry and the bodies not sunk deeply enough. The jackals have been at some of them. Still, that is nothing new to us.

Sayer has dropped out of the troop. He pretends his saddle has slipped; I think he is trying to get beyond the sight of the troop leader. An Arab village nearby is probably the object of his attention. We watch him for a few minutes, then forget his absence till he returns nearly half an hour later. His horse is lathered from galloping to catch up. He pulls into the section ahead and shows something under his blanket roll. I can just see the tip of some feathers. He has more foresight than we others; most of these Arab villages have a few old fowls, mangy, but eatable for all that.

Our new camp looks more promising than the last, it is near a Jewish village surrounded by an orange grove. We will attend to the grove later; I can see a lot of us will be in hot water over that grove. The oranges look most enticing and are something we have not had for years except at Jaffa, a few weeks back.

We have just been listening to the regimental orders being read out, as is done almost every day. Of particular interest is mention of thefts at a canteen the night before last. They asked those who knew anything about it to step forward. No one does; it is not expected that anyone would.

I had gone across to railhead that night for reinforcements coming up from the details, four others were there from different regiments, all bound on the same duty. The train had been late and did not arrive till two o'clock in the morning. We arrived before midnight and it was whilst waiting for the train that we conceived the idea of entering the canteen. Thought of the good things inside intrigued us immensely.

The fact that we intended taking what was not ours was of little consideration. What soldier has not done the same on countless occasions?

A careful survey revealed a surrounding network of barbed wire and a vigilant sentry, not at all loath to talk away the monotony of his shift, whom I engaged in conversation. Two others secreted themselves at a distance to guard against unexpected prowlers whilst the remaining two sought means of ingress. The canteen was a large canvas tent with two poles and canvas sides sunk well into the sand. The sand carefully dug away and the flap lifted, one man entered whilst the other replaced the flap in position so that, should the sentry continue his round, he would not observe what was afoot.

A few minutes and a case was passed out to be quickly smuggled away into the dark; two more cases came out; then the man from inside. They smoothed out the ground and disappeared. Shortly I heard the pre-arranged signal, bade the sentry good-night and made for where we had left our horses tied to a truck. We waited till the train came in before opening the boxes. The details for some reason did not arrive, so we set out on the return journey, anxious to get as far away as possible before sharing the results of our raid. We hoped for canned fruit or perhaps jam, but as luck would have it, we found the last thing any soldier wanted, hundreds of little bottles of salty meat extract. Who wanted Bovril in hot weather like this? We thought so much of it that we left it there on the sand for anybody who cared to pick it up.

The expected details turned up last night. Reinforcements are always more or less a source of interest; one never knows who may arrive, old friends with perhaps a bottle of rum stowed away, or new hands all nervous. Amongst them was an habitual reinforcement who came up regularly when we were spelling, and evacuated when we again went into the line. He was known to everybody as Bernard, of a type found in every army, a likeable fellow, full of spontaneous wit and a source of constant amusement though a regular rogue. He arrived clothed in a massive rabbit-skin coat which someone at home with little idea of climates had sent him. Performing drunken antics in this huge jacket he looked like a grotesque ape trained in circus tricks.

He was the original of a story which afterwards travelled the whole front and even as far as France. It has been told as happening in many places and more than one person has been cited as its hero. Whether it be a hero, scallywag, or just plain soldier trick, Bernard was the originator of it.

He had seen some whisky standing outside an R.T.O.'s tent under armed guard. To gain possession of a case he walked into the tent and asked the R.T.O. what time a certain train left. Being informed, he walked to the entrance, placed his hand on a case then called to the officer inside 'Will I get it from here, sir?' On being told 'Yes,' he calmly picked up the case and walked off into the dark. To the officer the enquiry meant the train, to the guard a case of whisky.

Amongst the reinforcements are many who are new; in fact most of them are, so we'll have to set to and teach them their business. How to pack a saddle so that the weight is evenly distributed and balanced not to sore a horse's back; to value water more than anything they possess; to drink it wisely and not just whenever they feel thirsty; that tea is the best drink of all; to try always for a quart pot in the mornings when on the road, and then fight down thirst till such times as another may be obtained, or till night time; the valuation of cover; to know that from a distance a man is invisible behind the slightest rise in the ground and how to dispose themselves to the greatest advantage when under fire and make full use of the natural formation of the ground. In fact the whole gamut, that has taken years to learn, we try to drill into them in a few weeks.

We often forget that once we were raw and did not know these things and perhaps, with the superiority of old soldiers, have a little contempt for these new fellows. We always hope to see the old hands come back, men who have been away wounded or sick. No matter how much theory may be imbibed in the details it amounts to little under actual service conditions; a certain element of danger always lies in a new, and to some extent unskilled, soldier.

We have plenty to keep us occupied during the days; we are even called upon for bayonet practice, as if we had not been taught all about this long ago. But the Army believes in keeping its hirelings occupied. However, we manage time for football, particularly when a rum issue is likely. The troops play each other for their share. Often the players know little or nothing about the game, merely playing to defend their rum issue.

Last week our troop won two successive matches, and no rum arrived. The following two nights we had it in succession, and knowing this in advance we saved both till the second night, when each man averaged five nips, allowing for those who did not use theirs. Five army rums, as we get it, are enough to turn an ordinarily quiet person into a wild man. That night bore testimony to this: next morning half the bivouacs were wrecked, and numerous swollen faces were about.

X——— was sent away this morning with pox, caught from one of the Arab women in Jaffa. He had managed to have some medicine brought up by a mate gone on leave and had been trying to cure himself, but our new medical officer found him out. X——— makes the third to go away since Jaffa. None of them reported themselves because of the stringent regulation regarding this form of illness. The patient is sent to a special hospital near Cairo, and during his incarceration receives no pay. Treatment lasts usually about two months; but pay is stopped at the full rate, not the portion drawn on service, so that usually it is five or six months without any money. This is the greatest hardship that can be imposed, which is why so few report themselves.

Life here is very good, we have never had a better rest camp. The oranges were especially appreciated but they are nearly all gone now: just a few holes through the hedges are evidence of our nocturnal visits. The Jews complained about this but the High Command always compensates, because they desire to impress the inhabitants favourably: they have an eye to post-war occupation of this country.

At night times we mostly play cards, being dependent on ourselves for all amusement. We see by slush lamps, made by inserting a piece of flannel in some bacon fat or dubbin; the fitful glare is sufficient to show the pips on the cards, if the wind is not too strong. One evening we had a visit from a band we had neither heard of nor seen before; we did not know that bandsmen would risk coming so near the line. They came mounted on donkeys, their instruments in a quaint little Turkish transport waggon that had been captured somewhere. We were more interested in their mode of travel than in the music, which doubtless was quite good. We found great amusement in watching them approaching from a distance on their diminutive mounts, legs swinging, almost scraping the ground.

We have been drilling in a new type of gas helmet; it does not leave the rotten taste in the mouth the flannel ones did, but is less compact and means just so much more gear to tie on our already overloaded horses. It is most unpleasant walking about in these things. First we have to put them on within six seconds, then we drill and go through manoeuvres such as happen when under fire. We do not take much interest in it; the whole thing is looked upon as something more to annoy us and take up our leisure hours.

Periodically we are lined up and the doctor examines our chests for scratches; he interprets that as a sign of lousiness. It was through this that he found X—— had the pox.

What a tediously monotonous business this constant delousing is! Especially when one has hundreds of them and each has to be killed separately. Our thumbs ache from the constant crack, crack, crack. Lenny says he has a particularly fine brand, an officer breed; he caught them from the sergeant-major who is always crawling to his betters.

It is nice and quiet sitting here in the shade. We have nothing to do but kill these pestilent little creatures which constantly torment us. Winn has taken his pants off to get at the inside of his trouser leg; they get very active there.

We are all practically nude and sit in our shirts, working down the seams, all except Smith. He is lazy today and has only pulled his pants down and is using a hot wire, as he thinks he can kill more this way. Lenny playfully throws a boot at him which knocks the hot wire against his belly. Smith howls, throws the boot back and asks Lenny if he wants to burn him.

We sit in silence for a time till Winn breaks the spell, asking Smith what he would do if the war were suddenly to end. To Smith, soldiering is but another way of earning a livelihood; a risky one admittedly, but whilst he is a soldier he is fed and clothed and has money in his pockets and no worries except that he may be killed, and that really is no worry for the dead know nothing about it. To be maimed is certainly not pleasant to think of, but men of Smith's calibre don't worry themselves too much about serious matters. Happy-go-lucky by nature he has gravitated into the army as a matter of course. The only problem that peace will confront him with will be finding another job. He and Lenny are somewhat akin in that respect; the pair of them would probably have one long holiday till their deferred pay was gone, and not till then would such things as their future livelihood interest them. Peace is great to think of; there are so many things one could do; but for the most part it is idle castle building though a pleasant subject of which to dream.

Lenny points to Williams, sitting oblivious to the conversation aroused by Winn's question, a beatific smile upon his face. It is not difficult to guess what Williams thinks of, his thoughts are usually in the one channel and that always means women, which he admits now is the case when Lenny asks him.

Conversation veered around to Moses the interpreter, recently taken on the strength and often alluded to as the wandering Jew. Rumour said it was his sister's influence that had obtained him the position, he spoke little English. Smith said that next war he would be an officer and make it his job to select interpreters.

The story went that a few days after we encamped here, one of the lower ranking officers sought for female company to share his nocturnal hours. He discovered a comely villager and made an immediate impression on her heart. He found her so exhilarating that he was unable to keep his satisfaction to himself, so that brother officers not so well suited vied for her favours. She, being ambitious as well as complacent, transferred her affections to a much higher ranker than her first love. He found her so enticing that when the call for interpreters went out, he was induced by promise of further and undivided favours to exert himself on her brother's behalf. Because of this we always allude to Moses as the Major's brother-in-arms.

* * * * * * * *

Our spell has been very delightful. For once in our lives we have had enough to eat, even if we have had to pay for it; the oranges too were something to remember. Rumour, that half-truthful jade, has been busy again; a brigade inspection is ordered, and this is probably a prelude to a new advance. Life here has been quiet, with little to interrupt it. An occasional Hun plane has flown over and one of ours attacked it, but except for these aerial combats we have lived in tranquillity. We gunners rather welcome stray enemy planes. It is an opportunity to use up doubtful ammunition and saves a lot of work in cleaning and inspecting. The sand, if we are not careful, sticks to the cartridges and causes stoppages; this is too great a risk in the line, so that if it were not for the chance afforded by these planes, we would have to clean each separate shell.

The day of the inspection arrives. We have spent countless hours cleaning our equipment, rubbing rust off stirrup-irons and in other unnecessary labours; we are glad the day has come so that we will no longer have to do this needless polishing.

Early this morning Smith went into a Jewish village nearby with some dispatches; it was to be a great day for him, as he was yet to learn. He had often admired a winery at this village but it was impossible for a common soldier to gain admittance to such a sacred place. Today, after his letters were delivered, he rode down to the winery as one will, to look at something we want but know is forbidden. To his welcome surprise he found that the officer of the guard was an old friend of his at home. By this means he gained admission and was quickly amongst the vats, anxious to appease a dream of weeks.

With a withered old caretaker he moved from vat to vat, tasting first one, then another, till he was fully satisfied, which was not an easy matter for Smith. His only regret was the impossibility of taking any away, as this was rigidly forbidden.

Such is the delusion of wine cellars, that though he felt perfectly sober underground, the air outside made him muddled, and soon he found he was very drunk. Paramount in his thoughts rose a vision of the inspection, now almost due. With only this thought in his fuddled head, he spurred his horse back to camp, irrespective of the path he took as long as he was in time.

Coming over a rise he found himself amongst the deserted lines of a troop now on the parade ground. His pace was too excessive to steer a clear path so that he quickly became tangled with the bivouacs; one of them brought down his horse, but not before he had wrecked others. By some means, best known to those who are drunk, he managed to retain his bridle rein and clamber on his horse again. By now the animal was terrified, and with its ears back came tearing straight for the inspection, which was now taking place. Smith was just able to hang on its back and no more. With Smith just hanging on, it made for the horses it knew. These, unfortunately for Smith, were near the front, and before he realised what had happened he was amongst us, scattering line after line of well ordered soldiers from his path. He still had sense enough to know the gravity of the offence he was committing, so instead of allowing the horse to stop as it would now, he plied spurs and kept going over the nearest hill and out of sight.

Enquiry was made as to who had committed this frightful outrage but the few who recognised him kept their peace. It was presumed he belonged to another brigade, and so far as we knew the matter ended there. One man, however, though he made no effort to report the matter, made a mental note of it, and that was the sergeant. Smith will have a lot of fatigue duties these next few weeks.

CHAPTER 4

O' Jerusalem

The various units forming the division move out in a long winding line, stretching as far as the eye can follow. The war clouds for us are black again; there is thunder in the air; a little span of peace has drawn to its unwelcome close. Our troop is left behind to clean up the litter and rubbish. We stack it in a heap preparatory to burning.

The Arabs hang around and keep poking the fire, seeking anything they may find; they are like birds, attracted by little bits of nothingness; in many ways they are birds, a lot of them anyway—birds of prey. Constantly they pull our fire to pieces, so that we have to keep resetting it.

Someone finds a quantity of dumped ammunition. We throw this into the blaze and quickly the cartridges start exploding. The Bedouin is a coward and runs from the noise, fearing flying bullets. He is perfectly safe if he but knew it, bullets exploded this way will not fly without the rifle barrel to propel them. Usually the shells just split and burst, the bullets remaining fast; sometimes a bullet may come away. But I have never known anyone hurt by such misadventure.

Our scavenging done, we hasten after the column till we find our place, join in the line and ride on, guided by our fates.

We cross right over the plain to the foothills below Jerusalem and halt for the night; the day has been so fine we do not bother to erect our bivouacs, to our sorrow. During the night it rains very heavily, washing our possessions into the slush and mud which the ground underneath quickly became. Daylight finds us slouching about in the mud, looking for something to sit on, half asleep as we move.

We are delayed at the foothills for three days which we utilise mostly in grazing our horses. The first morning, as we are spreading out near some Arab crops, our attention is suddenly centred on a furiously riding figure, rifle in hand, bearing down on two Bedouins. The Bedouins, sensing or fearing the tragedy about to be unfolded in our midst, run towards an officer present, seeking his protection. The horseman, *Horsecollar*, as we subsequently discover he was popularly known, veers his course round and dismounts alongside this group of three, pushes the officer aside, and shoots one of the Bedouins through the heart. The second fled for his life, Horsecollar firing harmlessly after him.

Being nearest the fallen Bedouin I rush towards him, but he is already dead, the blood flowing from a hole in his back as large as one's closed fist, whilst the puncture in his chest is no larger than the width of a pencil. The officer by this has overcome his astonishment, and quickly has Horsecollar arrested and marched back to camp.

An inquiry is immediately held into his behaviour. Horsecollar says he was grazing his horse on the Arab crops when the two Arabs in question came up and beat him. It is contrary to official dictum to allow our horses to touch crops; but, as our regard for the horses is greater than for official orders, we very often disregard them in this respect. In a fit of temper through this beating, he was uncontrollable to the point of lunacy; when fully aroused, he returned to camp for his rifle. He said he had only a hazy idea of killing the Bedouin, and had done it in the heat of the moment, without premeditation. His only thought was to avenge himself, not to commit murder. He certainly has the welts on his back as proof of the beating.

The Bedouins offset this by stating he had stalked and raped one of their women; they admit the beating, which was in retaliation.

The woman is brought and medically examined, the doctor declaring it was possible that she had been raped, but many years ago. He would say that she appeared a piece of common property and that she would in all probability have satiated Horsecollar's desires for a small offering. On the other hand it was a possibility that Horsecollar in his passion had not thought of this but only to satisfy himself and may have used force. Strong men segregated from female association, as an army is, are liable to become unbalanced in their lusts; passions denied may become tempestuous in their violence, particularly in a case as this, where the soldier concerned was subject to mental unruliness. The doctor was inclined to favour Horsecollar, for he probably assessed the case from a human point and not the rigid military view. The suggestion of rape was set aside by the type of woman concerned, but whether Horsecollar was guilty or not remains undecided; suffice it that he is on his way to Aden with two years to serve. Years spent in that unholy hole shorten a man's life. One does not live there: one exists, or dies. It is a hell amongst prisons, where the barbarisms of the middle ages linger, where a man is put on the treadmill amongst other tortures; exists beyond hope of reprieve, and, if he withstands the torments, eventually emerges with years cut off his life.

In the eyes of military law, Horsecollar had been guilty of a serious offence in that he had used violence against a native; the fact that it was a native probably made his case worse, for it seems very doubtful if he merited such severe punishment. The army engenders our hate for these nomads who constantly thieve and pillage from us. We are forbidden to lay a hand on them no matter what they do; they are free to rob and waylay us without redress. If we lodge complaints, nothing ever happens, for the army is ever seeking their goodwill. They are aware of this and play on it. It is because of this condition of affairs that we so often take matters into our own hands and settle them our way. More than one has been quietly dropped by riders on a screen, at a safe distance from official observation.

****

The tortuous ride up to Jerusalem occupied two days, along a road dangerously narrow in places and edged by sheer drops.

We encountered at one of these places a camel train which, however, gave us the right of way, and moved themselves higher up the hillside. One man ahead mounted on a great raw-boned roan very nearly slipped over. His horse frightened by the camels, as so many of them are, backed to the road's edge till it had one hind foot dangling over. The fright at feeling nothing to support it caused the animal to rush away from this new danger, through the camels it had so feared, and career to the ridge top where it stood quivering with terror. The rider dismounted to pacify the horse but nevertheless had to wait for the entire convoy to pass before he was able to regain the road.

We passed many graves, both British and Turkish, testifying to the bitter struggle that had been waged through these hills to gain this road we now passed in peace. The Tommy infantry had been sorely tried first to gain a footing and then to hold it and push on. We never cease to admire these brave little fellows, gallant prototypes of the bulldog that never lets go, who could be still more gallant if their officers were more in keeping with them.

The English idea of supplying officers according to one's birth and influence, with less attention to capabilities, savours a little of the feudal system of lord and master and loses much good. The practice of granting commissions to men without service, over the heads of veterans, tends to create weak leadership and does not engender the spirit necessary between officer and man for successful results. By this method experienced rankers, skilled in warfare, are placed in the hands of callow youths who know a good deal less of their duties than the men they command. Is it to be expected that they will know how a certain position is to be attacked, simply because by birth they are what they are? Coming into battle as officers without any previous introduction to warfare, they cannot conduct themselves to the best interest of their command and many lives must be lost unnecessarily whilst they gain that experience. Something perhaps could be learned from the Colonial idea of granting commissions in the field. By this means only original officers came from home, those created later are created by virtue of the knowledge and capacity they display in action. They must know their business in order to gain rank. This obviates schoolboys being given care of men with greater skill than themselves.

To pursue the subject. Is it fair that men in the ranks should be passed over, many of whom are good material and often better men by virtue of the fact that they are in the ranks and have not sought the elevation which, in many cases, they could easily have obtained? Is it fair that their lives should be unduly jeopardised so that boys and young men of position may carry their social position to war, where after all, everybody is one together on a common mission? Many of these youthful commanders consider it impossible to sully themselves by contact with the rank and file, others merely take advantage of conditions, seeing no reason to be a private when they can be an officer. Of the former type, very often the private is too good for them, that is if manhood counts for anything; and all is not a matter of social prestige. Many of these are too inclined to look on the ranker as so much dirt beneath their feet, which is why the Tommy could be even a better soldier with a better system of officering. It is the dirt of which he is made that supplies the *raison d'être* of their officers, it is this same dirt that makes possible glorious deeds, the reflected glory of which reacts to the advantage of the officer. This fact they seem either to forget or think impossible of consideration. All privates are not fit for commissions; but sufficient are, to supply the need. It is the principle that is at fault more than the men who advantage themselves by it.

* * * * * * * *

We entered the modern Jerusalem opposite the Jaffa gate, rode round the wall encircling the older city past the Damascus gate, and pitched our camp overlooking the Valley of Jehoshaphat and in a direct line with the Golden Gate. We had several days to wait here which pleased us immensely, providing an opportunity to view this wonder city of tradition. So much is expected from it that one must naturally be disappointed. It is an enlarged edition of other Palestine towns, peopled by a motley of divergent faiths and nationalities. Its difference lies in the walls, relics, and size and to some extent in its position, perched as it is on top of hills, but in a great degree also, in its Biblical associations.

The more one delves into its holy show-places, the greater doubt arises to confound one as to the verity of religion as worshipped here. Everywhere one is confronted by the apparent mercenariness of its priests, clamouring for alms with little more humility than the lowest beggar. Perhaps in other days it may be different; we soldiers represent a potential harvest; we come and go; they may not care so much about their conduct with us. Insults roll off their backs like water, if the clamoured offering is bestowed. But not all are like this, many conduct themselves with more stately mien, merely asking, never supplicating. The majority of the priests nevertheless are keenly alive to the possibilities of alms; the high, no less than the low, will refuse no gift.

With Smith and some others I went the round of historical sights. At the Holy Sepulchre a service was in progress; we waited till it finished, when a priest conducted us amongst the places of note. He showed us a reputed piece of the Cross; for this to be in existence at all is impossible, especially amongst such a crew, who would have bartered it long ago. Coming to a stone dedicated to the Virgin, the priest lit a candle and placed it in a niche. For this we were asked to pay: it was not suggested that an offering be made; the priest simply asked as he would for a fee, irrespective of our not having suggested or agreed to the candle being lit.

We saw the many and varied things of holy associations; the more we saw, the greater to me appeared the sham. The very slab on which Christ was laid is still extant, despite the fact that the city of His day lies buried beneath what even now is known as the old city. We learned that so great is the holy fervour shown at some of the functions frequented by pilgrims from many lands, that a number are always trampled underfoot. The inspection ended, the priest asked his fee. One is shown around, not with any suggestion or idea of propagating his faith, but for the fee he collects in so doing. Truly the troops are a harvest to them. The more I see and the more I listen to the priests, the more firmly I become convinced that the Churches' greatest enemy is education. I have been asked to believe many things, I am shown many things, and expected to believe all I am told about them. I am informed of these things as being facts, not possibilities. For years pilgrims have listened and believed to be true these very same things. The priests have not considered that amongst us may be many whose education requires that these stories be dressed in a different fashion. These pilgrims, with little learning, lean blindly upon their spiritual guides; if they are told it is so, it is. The Church through the ages has always been accepted and believed, its teachings accepted without question. With an era of more advanced knowledge, a lot of these beliefs must go into the limbo or else the Church will.

Moving from place to place one employs different guides: now it is a Christian, next a Moslem. Explanations are according to the creed of the guide. If he is a Christian describing Moslem relics, he will say 'The Moslems believe so and so happened here,' but if telling you of Christian things he will tell of them as a fact. The Moslem tells you the same.

Out of this mass of contradiction and corruption (and Jerusalem is very corrupt), the one thought to perplex me is which are the more to be believed, Moslem or Christian, Jew or plain heathen? I feel that as much truth lies in Moslem beliefs as in Christian or Jewish. To one reared in Christianity, the exponents of that faith as practised here are as abhorrent as the thought that amongst this mass of doubt thrives the plant of our faith. I find more zeal amongst the Moslems than the Christians and a far more earnest desire to show their faith and its visible symbols.

The lowly Moslem is always seeking alms, one associates that supplication with them. Here in Jerusalem, the Christian priests are also alms-seekers, more intensively so than the Moslem priests. I saw through the Mosque of Omar and listened to the Moslem beliefs with less suggestion for alms than had been the case in the Christian citadel of the Holy Sepulchre. The suggestion para-

AUSTRIAN TROOPS LEAVING JERUSALEM (GERMAN PHOTOGRAPH)

EL KANTARA ON THE SUEZ CANAL—20 MILES FROM PORT SAID—
MARKS THE SPOT OF THE ENTRY TO SINAI DESERT

mount above all else (as it appears to me) is the eternal call for charity—to give, give, give. In contrast, these two faiths present a peculiar divergence. Moslems are the same the world over, their faith does not vary but we cannot say that of Christianity; one has but to see worship here to understand that. This eternal call for charity seems to be the priests' first and last thought: one's religious welfare concerns him only in as much as he can extract.

It may seem that my eye is jaundiced, that my perspective is biased, but in reality my mind is very open. I have read my Bible and know its teachings; I wish to follow and accept its doctrines; I am not oblivious to that phrase 'Seek and ye shall find'; I have sought and I am seeking, but what I find is not that which I wish. Religion is something I have accepted without question, the creed of my fathers as passed to me, I accept it as they have done and strive to hold it.

The War has swirled me as a small integral part into this maelstrom which moves with such quickness that certain essentials of Christian teaching are omitted from one's daily life, in contrast to the attention paid them at home in the quietude of peace. I wish to accept and believe my faith; have brought it with me as a help and guide. The more I become involved in this seething atmosphere of death and pain, hope and sorrow, the greater grows my doubts as to the verity of many of my Biblical teachings. Jerusalem is the pivotal point of two great faiths, the Christian and the Mohammedan. Both are closely allied to it by tradition, precepts and teachings. Both faiths claim it as, incidentally, does the Jew. Yet this city of glory and holiness is a bed of sin, iniquity and insincerity, full of brothels, the low order of which I have never seen eclipsed, not even in Port Said before the war. The priests exploit it for worldly gain, they batten on us almost as much as does the lowly Arab. Each aspires to the one object, to gain what he can.

Contact with death (and I have looked death in the face, and have gambled with my life as with something inconsequential) gives one a much altered perspective from that retained by the man who lives in the tranquillity of his home.

Somehow this death and desolation and the kindred pains of warfare have altered my view, have altered it forcibly, for I have clung to my beliefs. To be so close to the threshold that the difference is infinitesimal, leaves one possessed of a much altered mental perspective.

I feel that the solace and help which my creed should offer is insufficient. I know that I am being drawn away from it, that its preachings to me now are not the glorious things they once seemed. I have striven with my soul, argued against what I have seen and know; I want my faith preserved; I want to retain it; it is my sheet anchor; without it I am lost. But strive as I may, the doubt is ever increasing. I had looked forward to our coming here, hoping that the associations of this Holy of holy cities would discredit my many doubts, that it would provide a support. It does not.

It has shown me another phase of Christianity, new to me, and made the struggle more difficult. I can feel the mental unrest and doubt that are gradually taking hold of me. One should not think too much about the things we see here or reason matters out; it is because I do this that I am losing faith. I am looking under the surface. I am slowly sinking into a morass of uncertainty and doubt which tears my mind. A little doubt of small matters is breeding a great doubt of larger. The more I reason the less I understand, the farther down I slip, till I feel I am releasing my grip on all that has been so dear. The Church should eschew war, for it is harmful and contrary to its teachings.

CHAPTER 5

Into the Jordan Valley

Smith is very happy this morning. He has been recounting a successful encounter he had with some military police last night. His care-free and happy-go-lucky nature leads him into much trouble, but he usually extricates himself; very little worries this hard-bitten rover. His whole life has been a wandering adventure. He has been in the war since nineteen-fourteen and was through Africa too. To him the world is a playground, nothing is serious, he takes life as it comes, has no worries and never worries. He has never married; a nature like his would never settle to it and I have never heard him speak of relatives. He once told me that his mother was but a dim memory and he never knew or heard of his father. Since he was a toddler he has fought and struggled, first for existence, later as a matter of course. He has been most things during the nearly fifty years of his life. Soldiering to him is but a livelihood; he has sailored too and covered as much the world as any man.

He is a good friend, with a knowledge of life vastly amusing and instructive. I don't know what occupation he has set down on his enlistment papers, but *philosopher* would be the most suitable. His merry eyes always see the good in life, twinkling from under a prominent brow, which is however almost unnoticeable in profile, as his hawk-like nose projects to such length. The skin on his face is wrinkled and tightly drawn, throwing his high cheek-bones into relief. It is his eyes one always sees, softening a face otherwise inclined to be hard, though not harsh. Streaks of grey show through a jet black poll surmounting a long lean body, all six foot in length, but with little flesh on it though not wanting in muscle. His long arms and very large hands suggest strength. He walks with a springing swinging motion, the latter probably picked up on rolling decks. Great strength lies in that rugged torso. I have often wrestled with him, and know the power of his bear-like hug, perhaps more ape's than bear's.

That he would use this strength of his against the military police we have had much evidence, and evidence too of the delight it always afforded him to score against members of that iniquitous organisation. His escapade of last night was as pleasing to us as to him, the police being detested and despised by all.

The women of easy virtue in Jerusalem are no better than their surroundings. Congregated in a few mean houses, they live in squalid depravity. It matters little to them whom they consort with; money is all they seek. In the presence of soldiers a request from a native would be greeted with vituperation, but acceded to were no soldiers present. This area is out of bounds, and no one with much self-respect would frequent it except out of curiosity. Smith wandered down there last night. He says he did not set out with that intention, but went that way by chance, with no idea of visiting the women.

Standing opposite one of the houses, he was observed by a police patrol. The fact that he was in the street mattered little; he was within the area, and to their way of thinking just as culpable as if actually inside a house.

Seeing trouble looming large ahead, he dived through a doorway, hoping to escape into a back street, but became lost in a maze of passages and rooms. Seeing a light under a door he burst in, to be greeted by a choice mixture of English and Arabic from the loving pair he had disturbed. Mention of the police stopped its flow, the soldier diving under the bed and Smith on top of a wardrobe, whilst the woman shrilly demanded what the police meant by their invasion of her room. Her talk was so much camouflage; they quickly forced their way in, searched around quickly, and found the luckless fellow under the bed. Hauling him forth, two escorted him away, his nether garments in his hand. Three remained to make sure no one else was in the room.

Smith must have moved or in some way attracted their attention, for despite his concealed position he suddenly found himself confronted by a face peering over the top near his feet. Possessed only of a desire to escape and without thought of consequences, he lashed out with one foot, catching the face full and knocking the policeman to a heap on the floor. Jumping up from his hiding-place he saw the two momentarily undecided, one in the act of tending their companion.

Leaping from the wardrobe, he caught the standing one full in the chest completely disabling him. Seizing a chair he swung, at the remaining Redcap and fled through the door.

* * * * * * * *

We can hear the crash and thunder of the guns in the valley below, not half a mile away as they bombard the Turkish line strung along the Jordan's edge. Our infantry must break through here before we can enter the oncoming advance. This swiftly flowing stream is strongly held, providing very formidable opposition; the ambulances that pass tell us this. When the river position falls the infantry will erect bridges for us to cross and then draw back, their task done, whilst we carry the fight to the plateau on the far side.

We lie secreted among the foothills which run in serried rows up and back to Jerusalem some twenty miles in our rear, from where we moved two days back. The heat is terrific, penetrating the poor shelters we have erected against it. The hills are a whitish brown gravel substance, devoid of vegetation, and reflect the sun rays with blinding intensity. Our only source of water is more than a mile distant, down a gully which is reached by a very narrow track, so narrow that we have to lead the horses in single file. It is very arduous work drawing water; the sun is trying and fatiguing, which adds to our difficulties in negotiating this narrow path. It is our first taste of the dreaded valley of which we have heard so much. We thought Egypt hot, but it is cool by comparison.

The air is charged with that intensity which always precedes a new advance; but that is not all. We have the heat and disease of this ill-omened place to contend with. A place of pestilence which, in the summer now drawing on, is regarded as uninhabitable for white men. The air is so still as to be uncanny, seeming to forebode evil—yet perhaps we think too much of the valley's reputation.

We are strong and healthy, rested and recovered from the exhaustion of past hardships. Inured to privation, we know how to thirst and starve, we can live on what would make ordinary men ill. Often we have existed on insufficient and bad food, thirsted for long stretches or slaked our parched throats on tainted water. We are hardened and capable of withstanding almost anything: events have tended to breed in us an alleviating philosophy. For this old world is full of sorrows and each of us only makes contact with a few of them, and plenty there are whose troubles are worse than our own. It is better that, instead of bemoaning the sorrows we meet, we rejoice because of those that pass us by.

****

The Turkish resistance had been stubborn and determined, sorely trying the infantry and costing many lives before a bridge spanned the river. The infantry packs had attracted the enemy machine-guns as the two lines lay exposed, out of trenches, and caused many casualties.

Moving in the dead of night, we rode in absolute silence across the valley floor to the Jordan *wadi* bed. The river is no more than thirty yards across at the point of our crossing. A pontoon bridge had been placed in position, between the two sides, sufficiently wide for man and horse abreast. We dismounted and led our horses in single file, the bridge rocking and swaying as the swiftly flowing stream buffeted it. Somebody a little ahead of me overbalanced, and plunged into the waters below, to be carried many yards down stream before he could beat the current to the shore.

It was a tiring, endless business moving a division in this manner, and occupied the whole night. When at last it was finished, we continued our ride across the flat to the foothills opposite where we had started. It is eerie in the valley at night near the Dead Sea. Uncanny lights and sounds come across it. Probably troops of both armies away down its sides. We would hear peculiar noises which we could not trace or explain, nor could we understand the lights we saw out on the waters.

All day we remain close up under the foothills, secured from observation from above and awaiting another night to provide sheltering darkness for our further advance.

We sit about, shelter from the blistering sun as best we can, chasing the shadows of our horses to avoid the hot rays. Often we have lain like this, holding our horses, bridle reins, whilst they fossicked for grass. If we lay in their path they would always step over us but never on. We have slept at nights holding our horses like this; they would move about, in the morning perhaps be standing right over us, but never have I known anyone to be much hurt by it. Today Johnson's horse felt differently about it, and stepped on the side of Johnson's head, tearing his ear away.

We watch the sun set and darkness fall, then in a long snake-like line commence our upward climb to the plateau. The only passage ways are by goat tracks, narrow and precipitous as such tracks are; the only road-way to this region, farther up the valley, is still held by the Turks.

For miles these paths wind, very often no more than a foot wide, in places so steep our horses could barely climb them. Sometimes we can ride up the grades, more often we walk ahead leading the horses, or else come behind hanging to their tails to help us up. Many times we wind around a precipice on a path but two feet wide: a slip would mean crashing to death many feet below. The climbing is at an extremely steep angle always leading up.

Some time before midnight the rain comes, falling in torrents and chilling us to the bone after the excessive heat of the past few days. The paths are now growing very slippery and the track becoming more difficult to negotiate.

For hours we climb, ever since sunset last night, and now it is almost day. I am tired and weary but struggle on half blinded, feeling most of my way, hanging on for the hourly spell almost due. The rain has penetrated my greatcoat, it will be through to my skin very soon. I shiver as if I have the ague; this sudden change of temperature goes through one like a knife. Around me are miserable-looking figures, stumbling along; sometimes somebody falls over a stone, and no one speaks - but not because of orders! Yesterday we had been sweltering in one hundred and twenty degrees of heat, this morning we shiver in forty degrees of cold. It might be forty below, we could not be any colder if it were.

At last the hourly spell arrives. I notice a depression in a rock nearby: it looks comfortable, what matter if it is full of water? I flop down into it, too tired to notice or care about the water as it penetrates the last dry bit of clothing I wear. I am asleep before I have properly settled, and awakened again before properly asleep.

Dawn finds us out on the plateau top but no sign of the enemy; he has probably retreated to better cover than this country affords. The ground is all slush and mud, nowhere that one can rest, and we are to stay here till night again. A number of loose stones lie about, and I collect some and place them in the mud to provide an elevation large enough to support my body. On this crude bed I lie down with my waterproof over me, so that the rain runs off and gurgles away between the stones under me.

The greatest hardship of the desert is now about us in abundance, water; I would like to turn some of it into tea to warm my vitals, but the few bits of wood are too wet to burn. How often we have prayed to exchange heat and thirst for water and cold; now that our desire is granted it is of no use.

With darkness we move on again, riding through the night in pelting rain. With the goat tracks behind, the country is opening out and allows more freedom of movement. It is difficult to keep awake, and I am perpetually dozing, depending on Blackboy to keep with the column. I do this once too often, and waking with a start find I have lost touch with the column. Standing still

I can hear nothing but the swish of the rain. Which way to ride I am uncertain, so I trust to Blackboy's instinct. When I do meet the column again it is with a strange unit, who cannot direct me to mine. For almost an hour I ride alongside seeking my regiment, meeting others similarly lost.

Soon after daylight we make contact with a Turkish patrol. They are few and we many, so we easily account for them. A little later an enemy plane swoops down and turns his machine-gun along the column.

Towards midday the many units separate and manoeuvre for positions preparatory to the attack. A few shells pass over in the afternoon but do little harm. Night comes and all is comparatively quiet. I find myself a bush over which I lay my waterproof, it is full of prickles but they do not penetrate through the sheeting, and form a mattress, to my tired bones more comfortable than any feather bed ever was. Banks and Miles are nearby, the latter having taken Stone's place on the gun. Another troop is supplying our outposts tonight, for which we are thankful as we can rest in a measure of peace.

****

At daybreak we move forward over a small depression and draw the fire of the enemy guns. They are mostly five-nines charged with high explosive, and we can only reply with mountain batteries, as the way in was too difficult for anything of heavier calibre, and we shall be without larger guns till the road is cleared to permit their access.

Passing over the flat, we ride under the shelter of a low cliff, dismount and await orders. Two Arabs appear on a hill behind, waving a cloth of some kind which is suspiciously like a signal: somebody drops them with a rifle. All the Arabs this side of the Jordan are armed and professedly friendly towards us, but there are many of doubtful sympathies such as these two.

An order comes along to man the ridge, machine-guns to take all ammunition-panniers. That means warm work. I linger for the few moments needed to buckle up the pack, and then follow in their wake. As the troop appears on the ridge the men come under very heavy shell and machine-gun fire which completely impedes further advance, necessitating our holding on here as best we can. To my right I see a stone sangar, remnant of bygone Roman days; it suggests good shelter, which I profit by.

We are strung out in a long line along the hill top and, being a few yards behind, I can see them all quite plainly. A five-nine is making us its particular target, working along our sector with uncomfortable regularity and precision. After a little my ears become attuned so that I can tell where each shell will fall. This is very nerve-racking; I feel fidgety and can see others squirming about.

The Turk has our range too close for safety and is getting even more exact. We cannot move either forward or back, his machine-guns spray us if we raise ourselves. We are in an awkward corner and it looks like getting even worse.

A five-nine explodes at the far end of the troop line; the next one is nearer to me; another comes still closer; they are working along in quick succession till one drops a mere twenty yards away. The firing then moves back to the other end. I am glad to be at the end of the line and not in the middle; they get it both coming and going there.

Back again comes the gun, I can tell by its whine where the shell will burst. I know that one in each sweep will fall near where I am. As it works away the tension relaxes till again it comes my way, making me shrink into myself and causing an involuntary tightening of the muscles. As it rushes down in a deafening shriek I cringe to the ground, striving to make myself as small as possible, holding my breath whilst my heart dilates and throbs. As it completes the parabola I grip my mouth, closed, and lie tensely waiting, expectant.

It bursts so near that I distinctly hear the vicious ping of the flying splinters. The relaxing strain, as they pass harmlessly by, gives one the feeling of having been rescued from drowning, and one is assured of another five minutes before the gun works back again. As it does, I go through the same agony of expectation and doubting dread, the same feelings which bring the sweat out all over me.

As the explosions work away I watch fascinated to where I expect the next detonation to be. It comes, and with it a scream. As the smoke clears I see Williams clutching his leg, an agonised expression on his face. His knee cap has been completely blown away. The next explodes harmlessly, and another too. The following one falls short on the far end of the line, the smoke clears and reveals a hole where a few seconds before had been a man, now there are only a few shreds of flesh and cloth. Pieces of bone and flesh thrash down on us as the stretcher bearers are dragging Williams away. They lie down as this shell bursts, then continue their crawling; no need to worry about the fresh casualty -there are only bits to be picked up.

With the shortened range our position becomes untenable, the roar is deafening. I listen for the next one but cannot tell where it will fall; my ears are drumming from the last; the concussion of it has jarred me like a blow. Back comes the inevitable sweep, after the last burst I fully expect to get this one. It bursts so near that bits of stone from the sangar hit me and the concussion sends me into a daze, so that I can't reason properly and my thoughts turn in a chaotic meaningless jumble, rushing through my mind in a kaleidoscopic tangle.

Only one idea, one tangible thought, is clear; it is my hour. I have expected death before, have waited for it to reach out and take me; this feeling now possessing me is not new. It is the inactivity, lying quite still, unable to move, just waiting and expecting, that is more terrifying than death itself. Death is nothing, coming so quickly that one knows nothing of it. Fear comes not from the thought of death but from the suspense that precedes it, which pounds in our brains with maddening intensity, the fear of the unknown. I would far sooner take my bayonet and charge into the unknown than lie here waiting, anticipating, expecting, inactive.

I know the next shell will fall where I lie; it is not terror which makes me think this, but my experience of gun-fire automatically registers in my brain where to expect the burst. I am afraid (who isn't?) but not terrified, and I am afraid because it is humanly impossible not to be.

I hear the whine of the shell as it shrieks towards us in increasing intensity. I lie quite still, it cannot be escaped, I just lie and wait. The same feelings pass over me as each time a shell has burst near. Again the muscles contract, my mouth sets, my heart swells so that I cannot breathe. It is coming! From a whine it has grown to a shriek, it swoops down in a crashing crescendo, its shriek loud in my ears so that the drums must break. It seems as if the shell itself is in them. As it completes its course it ends in a flash of blinding flame which envelopes me, swirls me up, then allows me to sink down and down and down.

I travel at a seemingly terrific speed into a void, sinking in a pit which has no ending. Rushing down and down, surrounded by a brilliancy of light that is part of me and travels with me. The sides of the pit keep rushing out and hitting me with painful force, then recede from sight, the impact showering me with myriad sparks. An odour of burning is in my brain, an elusive smell which vaguely I have smelt before but what it is I cannot tell. It is sickening and nauseates my stomach; but my stomach doesn't seem to be part of me. This is strange, but neither do my head or legs or anything. I look about and see my various members separately rushing down. I have disintegrated. That is puzzling, for at the beginning they had all been together, I was a whole body. Now it is as if I am a spectator, watching my own body flying into space. As I look, the pieces come together, and once again I am whole and part of them, only my stomach does not seem to keep pace, it is streaming away behind like a tail on a kite.

Peering down I see that the pit has a bottom; it is rushing up to meet me, but I too am moving, still sinking. It must be that we are coming together, and I steel myself for the impact. My stomach catches up. We are united again, but I am very sick and I want to vomit. The bottom is almost here, I stop breathing awaiting the impact, vomiting as I do, but strange thing, it is my stomach that I spew out. Taking my eyes from the upward rushing bottom to look at my stomach floating by, it hits me with painful force. The light that has been around me is dying, it

79

grows dim and fades away. I am part of the bottom of this limit-less void, it absorbs me, I am nothing, there is nothing, nothing exists, only darkness.

* * * * * * * *

The sun is past its zenith and sinks to rest. My head is throb-bing painfully, aching and drumming as if an expanding drum were inside it, stretching it out. I must have been here for hours; the sun, when last I remembered, was on the climb. I try to move away and avoid a smell that sickens me, but I cannot lose it: it is on my clothes where I have vomited.

How I come to be here I do not know, someone has dragged me down. Where the others are I don't know. I don't know anything except that my head seems to have gone mad. It goes round and round making me dizzily sick. I try to think, I re-member a shell and a sangar, yes a sangar; luckily it was there else I should be in hell now.

CHAPTER 6

Across the Jordan

It is foolish, I know, to wander in this direction for I may come into a sniper's view at any moment. But my attention is attracted by something lying on the ground a couple of hundred yards away. As I draw near I make out the lines of a body, and, thinking it may still be alive, I press on to make sure. When I am almost at it a burst from a machine-gun zips by like a swarm of angry hornets. Falling on my belly I crawl the last few yards to the body, and find it is still alive but no more.

Whoever he is, he has lain here some time, the ground is saturated with blood from a gaping hole in his side. The leg too is shattered at the hip and the arm on the same side broken. The leg is in a mess; I do not think it will ever be of use again. Tearing open the blood-clotted tunic I find that a piece of shell has torn the stomach, and what with the broken limbs and the sepsis that will shortly set in, life for him will be an agony till he dies, as die he must. If I drag him back to the clearing-station they will only try to patch him up, which means prolonging unnecessary agony with no hope of eventual recovery.

I am undecided what to do, and try to think as I plug his wounds. I try to carry him back, but his weight and the awkwardness of the fractures make this impossible. Still, I must try. The machine-gun finds us and fires a burst, and that prohibits my getting him back alone. One thought occupies me, a humane way out, but I am loath to adopt it. Still wondering what I should do, I get back to the lines and look for someone to help me. I do not know how he can be in this sector, unless he has been twice wounded. Returning with the first he may have been overtaken by the second, which has left him there unconscious.

Meeting two bearers I ask them to come back with me. It is fortunate, for the wounded are their care and they will be better able to help the poor devil than I.

They examine him but I know they will say he is done for. I can see it in their faces if I did not know it already. I say to them that perhaps it is a pity I have found him, better to let him die, that would be less pain than trying to mend him. They tell me it would take days for him to die, days of awful agony, better to put him out. It was as if they had read my thoughts, the idea which I was revolving in my mind, but I feel I cannot do it, the thought of shooting a man like this is abhorrent. Doubtless I have killed many of the enemy, but somehow that is different, the mind is in another key then and circumstances changed, but this broken body arouses in me a sympathy, a pity that I cannot overcome.

I look into their faces and fancy I see the same reluctance, no one speaks or moves, seemingly occupied by one thought. One of them takes a hypodermic needle and fills its little tube, I think with morphia. It seems to be a lot. I watch the needle inserted and the liquid forced in. I am not sure I understand and say that it looks a big dose. He replies that it is—too big.

* * * * * * * *

How cold it is tonight on the ridge! Machine-guns are racketing away on the right but our sector is fairly quiet; this is just as well, for there are not many of us left, far too few to hold it.

I was lying a little higher than the others, sniping at occasional targets. A bullet hits the rock I am lying on and ricochets over my leg. I don't need two warnings, so I change my position to a more sheltered one.

We are too sparsely scattered to offer more than a semblance of resistance should an attack come. The horses have been tied head to head so as to release some of the horse holders, for casualties have greatly thinned our ranks. Banks and Miles have been removed with wounds, Winn is dead and of Claude we know nothing. He was seen to fall, but beyond that we do not know. It is always the best who go.

We keep firing our rifles, but it is only make-believe, to create a suggestion for the Turks' benefit, that we are more numerous than we actually are.

We stand-to just before the first signs of day and watch the dawn as it gradually suffuses the country in a dull depressing glow. No warmth is in the sunrise, it suggests more of the rain which has constantly dogged us since we scaled the plateau. Troops like us don't take kindly to the cold, we are acclimatised to heat and our blood is thin.

Later in the morning a squadron from another regiment is joined to us; separately we are insufficient, but together we may manage to hold our sector. We'll have a damn hard try anyway, and it will not be too easy for the Turks if they come.

A convoy of wounded is awaiting an escort back to the clearing-station; Smith and I are attached for this duty, and also to gather in loose horses which are roaming the hills. We know all the animals in the squadron, which is probably why we are sent. The convoy is composed mostly of camels with those deadly cacolets slung each side. Some of the wounded are able to ride and are on their own horses. Though the Arabs around are assumed to be friendly, one never knows, and Turkish patrols are liable to bob up, so that an escort is really essential. The country is full of roaming Arabs, all armed. The rifles they carry are more varied than the colours of their clothes. They date back for many years to the old single-loading patterns with soft-nosed bullets, half an inch in calibre that would tear a great piece from anyone unlucky enough to be hit by one. Some carry the modern Turkish arm, and not a few our own Lee-Enfields.

****

Smith, who rides at the head of the column, has just taken a pot-shot at one of these nomads; he considered that the Arab was acting in a peculiar manner. He has a deeply-rooted hatred of these Arabs, for he was once ill-treated by some of them when overtaken on a lone patrol. Since then, if when riding on a screen or rearguard, he came in contact with any of these nomads and they did not quickly give a satisfactory account of themselves, he was liable to forget military orders and indulge in a private war of his own.

The Bedouins are like protected game. They pillage and thieve from us and sometimes do far worse, yet we are never allowed to lift a finger in retaliation, which aggravates our feeling towards them. We are told they are useful information carriers as they are allowed to pass between both armies. Probably this is true but if they are informers for us they are also for the Turks. More than once our positions have been indicated to the Turkish artillery, and beyond a doubt through their agency.

The only tobacco I have is deep in my saddle wallets and not easily accessible, so I ride along the convoy to borrow the makings from Smith. Towards the middle (there are probably thirty camels in the train) I notice one man with his head swathed. Through the folds of the bandage the blood was slowly seeped, showing like a small red dot; his face is whitish grey, suggestive of death. I feel his pulse beating very feebly. The shaking of the cacolet is gradually lowering the vestige of life remaining.

Coming up to Smith I asked for the tobacco I wanted, he handed me his tin and a leaf out of a Bible—it is the book of Job we are smoking. Someone had given him this Bible long ago, and he carried it about for some inexplicable reason, though he never read it. Running out of cigarette papers one day he had found the thin paper a good substitute, but care was needed not to smoke too much of it as the printing ink was liable to make one sick.

My cigarette burning, I drew aside to allow the convoy with its Egyptian cameleers to pass, at the same time watching for the man with the dotted head. Feeling his pulse again I cannot detect any movement. An hour later at the ambulance he was dead and was probably so when I last held his hand.

What a piteously desolate place the clearing station is! A few tents to house the more desperately wounded lying on the bare earth; whilst those with lesser injuries are scattered about outside, protected against the elements as best these harried medicals are able. Our train of wounded are not welcome, for the staff are overtaxed and unable to give proper attention to those already here. With many grumblings they set to work doing what they can, their grumblings meaningless nothings, for the wounded are far in excess of their facilities and the staff are near exhaustion and the end of their resources.

We help to remove the wounded from the camels, then before going in search of stray horses, wander through the tents seeking anyone we may know. In a corner huddled together I found both Miles and Banks, and feel much happier at seeing these two again. Smith followed me in and rolled a cigarette for each with a page from the inevitable Bible. They are not up to talking, but seem to relish a smoke. We tell what news we have, then quietly move out, dodging amongst the many forms lying on the floor. . . .

At the doorway a major grasped my arm. 'I want some one to help me,' he said, 'you look a hefty fellow—come in here, you too,' nodding to Smith. Lying on a crude board bench was an infantry captain in his shirt only. The trousers had been removed, revealing a shattered leg. When we had looked him over the medical major drew us aside and explained that the leg had to be trimmed, there was no anaesthetic left so it was up to us to hold him down with the aid of the only orderly he could secure.

Smith looked at me then turned to the doctor, telling him that it savoured a little of cruelty. Couldn't some other way be found, or someone else to do it? Apparently there was no other course left, so we decided that if the captain could bear it, we at least could help.

The doctor explained to the captain what was necessary, that if he was removed in his present condition he would probably not survive it. No objection being raised by the patient, we made the simple preparations required.

His good leg we strapped to the slab and threaded a padded rope across his stomach. Smith stationed himself by the leg whilst I placed my arms under his, locking them across his chest, whilst the orderly stood by.

The captain watched our actions with a look of supreme calm till all was ready, then turning his head towards the doctor he quietly told him to get on with it, the first words he had spoken. With the first cut of the scalpel in the living flesh, the captain gave a shiver and turned his head. I could see into his eyes. They stabbed into me like piercing orbs filled with a depth of agony that I shall not easily forget. I was overcome with an infinite pity for this man, mingled with an admiration for his courage such as few possess. . . .

******* *

It is spitting rain again as Smith and I ride up a hill in search of the horses we have to take back. We have not spoken since we left the hospital tent, each of us thinking of the captain. Smith voices his thoughts and remarks on the courage that allows a man to be cut about like that. He goes on to say that he knew we must help the doctor but he was a little diffident about it, that it was the cold-bloodedness of the thing. One didn't know the many things one would be called on to do when a soldier. In the last few days he had fought, helped with burial parties, held a man whilst his leg was cut off, and done a dozen other things that one never thinks about when one enlists. He asks me if I had done any burying.

'I helped with a couple, not our troop though,' I tell him.

'I'll bet the padre was not there to see you do it,' he rejoins.

'Not ours, Smithy, that fellow from the fifth said the words.'

'You bet he did, else there were no words said. The parties I was on, the padre was missing. He's nothing but a yellow-bellied hypocrite anyway. Damned if I know where he hides himself; if a few bullets are flying about it is useless to look for him to attend any burying. Always turns up though when any food is about. He's a great friend of the quack's.'

'The quack hates him worse than water without whisky.'

Our conversation is abruptly terminated by a fusillade of shots from behind an adjacent hill. In doubt of the reason for this, we decide to make sure, and spur our horses to the foot of the hill, dismount, tie them head to tail, and make up the incline.

Nearing the top, we fall on our bellies and crawl the last few yards. To our surprise, on peering over the ridge, we find a body of Arabs indulging in civil war. Some difference must have led them to fighting. Divided into two factions, they were swarming behind such cover as they could find, firing the meanwhile, probably no more than twenty all told.

Smith is half-inclined to join in, but I restrain him. Not that either of us has any compunction on firing on Arabs as Arabs go, but out here many of them are allied to Lawrence. Should some of these belong to his cause we might aggravate the political situation. On the other hand they may belong to tribes who have avowed their loyalty to Turkey, in which case our firing would have been for the good. But we have no means of settling this problem, so we content ourselves by taking a position as onlookers.

One party, endeavouring to outflank the other, pivots the fight away from where we lie. This perhaps is just as well, for they are dangerously near our position and may draw us in. As it is, we come very near it.

Two of them come round the base of our hill, evidently thinking to get behind their opponents. In doing this they find our horses. Smith is the first to notice this and quickly scuttles along the ridge to come in behind them in his turn. Seeing the horses, they halt in momentary surprise whilst I hide behind a rock near by. Peering round its edge, I see them going back in the direction Smith has taken, which means they will meet face to face. To check this, I wait till their backs are turned, then step out, and fire a shot over their heads to distract their attention.

They wheel about at the sound, and I cover them. Smith, perceiving what has happened, closes in with me, his rifle also directed at them. Unable to speak their language, we are doubtful of their feelings towards us. Not wanting to disarm them, and perhaps unwittingly help the wrong side, we find another way out.

Whilst Smith keeps them covered, I remove the bolts from their rifles, and this done, we both mount and ride away in the direction from which we came. Having covered about two hundred yards we halt, wave our arms to attract their attention, then drop the bolts where they can see them. Moving on again, we see they understood our action and are coming up to recover them.

* * * * * * * *

With some eighteen horses gathered, we look for somewhere to camp the night. Dark is falling and it is too late to return to the line; we probably would be lost at night. Remembering a feed dump we had seen during the day near the clearing-station, we make for it. Whose it is we don't care, for darkness will shield our marauding activities from the ambulance, should they be interested in them. Breaking open a bale of tibbin, we add some barley and feed it to the horses, the first decent feed they have had for days. As for us, we have nothing, so we set to work constructing a shelter from the rain, which is still falling in spasmodic showers.

For seven days we have been constantly wet, the few breaks in the weather being insufficient to dry our clothing. It is only that we are so hardened by the rigours of guerilla warfare that we are able to withstand the cold and not succumb to pneumonia or such like ailments.

Shivering with cold, and miserably hungry, we commence digging a circular trench within which we erect a shelter of sorts, using bags of horse feed. Insufficient materials prohibit a four-sided structure so we were exposed to the elements at one end. Over the top and draping down the gap in the sides, we place a blanket. Into this crude structure we crawl and lying on the damp earth try to sleep on what we are pleased to term our bed. We are too tired to worry about prowling Bedouins, or the possibility of the rain blowing in on us. As it is, we sleep huddled up, for our house is too short to permit of stretching full length. . . .

Some time in the early morning our shelter came toppling

in on us, pinning me right down, and I remained there with my head pushed in the mud till Smith was able to get out and extricate me. One of the horses had broken loose and his nibbling at the bags had caused them to fall. The barley and its dust clung to our wet garments where it had poured through the hole eaten away by the horse.

Struggling out we sat huddled with our backs against the bags and our behinds in the mud, cursing the elements, the war and everything that irritated us. Sitting this way the water soon seeped through our breeches, freezing us still more (if that was possible) till we finally gave up in disgust and contented ourselves by stamping about in the mud seeking to warm ourselves.

As soon as day appeared, we filled the feed-bags and prepared to return. In mounting, Smith pulled his horse down on himself, both rolling on the ground. Smith rose with the fresh mud sticking to him, and some manure as well. The horses had so felt the night chill that their legs were too numb to support us. To overcome this we walked them about for half an hour which restored their circulation sufficiently for us to mount and ride away. . . .

* * * * * * * *

Days go by and still we hang to this deadly line; we don't seem to gain anything, but irrespective of that, we are loath to leave it, for we have paid dearly to get what we have and natural cussedness—or call it what you like—incites us to stick and end properly what we have begun. . . .

One morning I go back with five riding-wounded to the dressing station at a village some few miles in our rear. Along a broken strip of roadway we pass a group of dead Arabs, probably a dozen of them. They have been fighting amongst themselves, as others were the day Smith and I encountered them near the ambulance. One has been ridden over and lies squelched into the roadway, his body members coming apart. Another lies with his head grotesquely pulled back, looking like a bobbin on a spindle except that it is no longer round: a horse's foot has squashed it. Two camels have also gone into the limbo of dead things. They do not seem to have been killed, but to have died from natural causes. Probably they slipped and fell on the greasy mud, sinking to the ground and dying where they sank—a way camels have.

A little farther along we come upon two German lorries, stuck fast and abandoned in the mud. Not a vestige of wood remains on them; every bit has been removed to make fires in this treeless desolation. The tyres are steel bands packed with wood, evidence of the pinch Germany is feeling.

Towards mid-afternoon we enter the village, where I quickly hand over my charges and, taking their horses, set out on the return journey. Passing a section of the light car patrol my nostrils are assailed by the tantalising odour of cooking food. It brings me to a halt. The little we have had for many days past has been scrappy and insufficient, and I feel very hungry. The cook, perceiving himself watched, turns to me and asks if I am hungry, he probably knows I am in from the line, where victuals are scarce.

This is too great a suggestion to pass and, assuring myself they have plenty, I soon repair the omissions of past days. They are able to carry plenty in their cars, so I eat my fill without fear of robbing others. It is only bully fried with onions, but it tastes far better than that.

We sit and talk for a time till I get up preparatory to returning. Seeing my intention, this newly-found friend strongly advises against it, as I shall have to travel part of the way by night, which is very risky these times in this country. It requires very little persuasion to tempt me into remaining till morning. The lure of a restful night and more food before leaving is too much for me.

* * * * * * * *

In the early morning we line out prior to evacuating this unfortunate sector. We are wearily glad to be rid of it, but bitter that we must evacuate; it looks to us mighty like defeat and we don't relish that. The High Command's explanation is that we only came up here to gain information, which having been successfully obtained, there is no longer need for our presence. If that be true, it has been exceedingly costly. We feel very sad as we ride along, everybody is leading spare horses, some two and three. Each empty saddle means a comrade passed on, but we hope some day to avenge all this. Should we come again we will repay.

Rations have come for the half-squadron which has been with us, but they having returned to their units, we must provide a guard till they return for them. To our troop falls this duty.

We know an evacuation is taking place but we are not as yet aware of its extent so that we sit about and talk, blissfully ignorant that we are between our own retreating front line and the Turk. Feeling hungry and thirsty we boil our billies, scraping up grass for the purpose. Having lost my pot, I wander afield seeking an empty can as substitute. Whilst thus occupied we hear a fusillade of rifle shots. The officer, believing it to be an enemy patrol, instantly calls us together to move on. I am doubtful of all this, thinking it probably some Bedouins indulging in one of their periodic scraps, but seeing I am liable to be left behind I hasten on and rejoin the troop.

Along the road, the same one I had taken a few days ago with the wounded, we pass a convoy of injured, awaiting horses and cacolets to take them back to the village. They have an armed guard, and as everything seems fairly safe our officer leads on.

A little later we pass another troop from our regiment returning with lead horses for these wounded. Not long after this we hear a second outburst of firing, this time near where we had left the wounded. Quickly after this two loose horses appear on the road without riders. This entirely alters the complexion of matters. It looks now as if it really had been a Turkish patrol we had heard.

Believing this to be the case, the officer leads us behind a low hill, where we dismount and await eventualities. It is not long however before a detachment of Turkish horse appears, probably twenty of them. We wait till they come close up before firing and are rewarded by seeing over half their number fall. The remainder wheel about and gallop back from whence they had come, we keep firing after them—speeding the parting guest.

We now hurry on back for assistance and return with a full

regiment, but too late. The wounded have entirely disappeared and with them the troop of lead horses.

★ ★ ★ ★ ★ ★ ★ ★

Back in the village all is bustle and hurry as the units ride out and down the tortuous roadway, far too narrow to accommodate but a portion of the troops here. Some go out by the goat paths but, fortunately, to us falls the privilege of the roadway, which is vastly easier riding.

All day we keep moving forward, accompanied by a streaming endless line of refugees who dare not remain. Some have shown friendliness to us, which may mean a Turkish bullet when we are gone if they did not flee themselves. Old men and women, little children and helpless babes, a streaming continuous line of fleeing humanity, for the most running away from Turkish vengeance. Many are glad to escape imposed conditions; what will become of them all or where they will go, nobody knows. They carry their belongings on their backs, a blanket enwrapping all their possessions, cooking utensils projecting through the folds. Some, but only a very few, have small hand-carts; for them the going is more difficult, but they are able to carry more. Our horses keep these carts pressed to the narrow winding roadside.

We constantly stop and dismount to help the unfortunate whose bundles have slipped, or perhaps an old man or woman, wearied under the weight of their years and the weights on their backs. We place a lot of the bundles on the lead horses whilst their owners hold to the stirrups; they cannot ride.

Most of these refugees are Christians of mixed nationalities, probably Syrian stock and in some cases mixed with Arab, or else of Balkan or Circassian extraction. They are mostly very old or very young; what has happened to youth we do not know, they probably are roaming the plains behind. They are different people from the roaming Arabs and Bedouins whose home is the limitless desert or plain. These are village dwellers and in consequence more timid of nature and devoid of the predatory habits and instincts of their wilder brethren, if breth-

92

ren they can be called. They are only brothers inasmuch as they inhabit the same country, by nature they are opposites.

We are not particularly interested in them as people, only sorry for their very evident distress which calls upon our pity, for which reason we help them. Most of them wear the charms so expressive of the Catholic faith and constantly show them to us. They think because of their Christianity they have a tie with us; we care little for that, creed is a matter of small importance. It is so difficult to repose much faith in Christian things these days, all is so openly opposed to Christian doctrines that we bother little about it.

Dotted along the wayside we see some of the more feeble, succumbed to the rigorous demands made on their weak bodies by this hurried flight. They fear our column will pass ahead and leave them struggling behind, a prey to the Turk who will shortly follow in our rear. We know a number cannot make the offered safety across the Jordan; they will drop and perish here where they struggle. Life is a precious thing, and we all fight for its retention. These old men who have lived their span, still fight on to live just a little longer. They are a down-trodden people, ground under the Turkish heel, and life for them is all hardships and little pleasure. What we choose to call the civilised world does not know the battle and struggle which these people call life.

It is night before we reach the valley where we debouch from the hills and circle under them till morning. At daybreak we move on again, across the Jordan, and form a new front line till destiny once more calls us into the maelstrom.

How the heat bites into us! The past two weeks have lowered our resistance. Poor old Blackboy is foundering, his legs can barely carry him. Each time we halt I have forcibly to drag him into movement again; it has all come on him overnight. The result of privations and sudden change of temperature. I am very weary and footsore and struggle along as best I can leading Blackboy; he would carry me but he is wretched enough without my added weight; a few days' rest will cure him.

Es Salt

Refugees fleeing from Es Salt

How different the valley is! Its heat roasts us, and we feel it so after the sudden change from the plateau, where all was wet and cold. We have never been dry once during those two weeks, always wearing our greatcoats; and, as the chill and wet gradually penetrate, we wrap our blankets about us.

In this spectral attire we have lived and gone about our daily duties, except when actually in action when we removed them because of the hindrance. Some wear Balaclava caps over their heads, but most of us favour handkerchiefs or cloths. I preferred a handkerchief about my lower jaw and a towel around my head turban-fashion, with my hat tied on top. Fortunately I have two spare pairs of socks which make excellent gloves. As it is my hands are cut and sore from leading horses who, each time we gallop, pull and strain on my numb fingers.

CHAPTER 7

Assault on the Plateau

Days go by to become weeks, weeks turn into months, the heat is terrific, and we grill in our own fat. The summer has reached its height bringing with it all the pestilence this valley seems to harbour. Malaria and its kindred parasitic diseases are taking toll of us whilst snakes and vipers, scorpions and spiders seem to be everywhere, and myriads of flies and mosquitoes batten on us; so that one constantly waves one's hand or a twig to keep these germ-laden creatures away.

We have a saying of Egypt that it is the land of sun, sand, sin, and sore eyes; very true from the troops' point of view. It may almost be said to apply here, though in somewhat dissimilar circumstances. The last two are missing, no woman being in this region, though many have sore eyes from the sun glare. As for sand, we have dust as a substitute: great clouds of enveloping choking dust. The sun is the same old fireball that glares down on Egypt, but is here intensified to an unbearable degree.

The valley lies between foothills, a flat expanse some ten miles across at the Dead Sea and tapering in as it runs north. Down its centre flows the quickly running Jordan, making its way like a tortuous snake, averaging about sixty feet in width. Through centuries of time it has gradually eaten its way deeper into the earth, so that in many places the bed is hundreds of yards wide though the actual stream may be no more than twenty.

Over everything lies a surface of dust, many inches deep,

which when stirred hangs suspended like a pall, providing a most effective screen for those who ride through it. The air is so still that smoke from a fire goes up to heaven; the only disturbances are dozens of willy-willies chasing each other like mischievous children. Powerful enough to lift small weights and drop them a few yards away, perhaps to snatch up a bivouac-sheet or a piece of clothing laid out to dry.

Besides two monasteries by the river, now deserted till the heat has gone, the only habitations are a few mud and stone hovels grouped together under the name of Jericho. Peopled by a handful of dried-out natives, it has nothing to suggest its one time Biblical fame and glory. The road down from Jerusalem forks through it, one arm crossing over the river, the other wandering into nothingness farther up the valley. This town, if town it may be called, nestles near the foothills, almost overlooked by the Mount of Temptation with its monastery perched high up the side, accessible only by a narrow winding path.

A few dust-laden bushes, stunted trees, and occasional patches of deadish yellow grass provide the only signs of vegetation, a negligible quantity. Higher up as we follow the disappearing road, little streams run down the hills, converging into *wadis* which feed the Jordan. They draw their waters from the heights which, by a quirk of nature, have rains that the valley never sees. Everything about this valley suggests that Nature was in humorous vein when she conceived it. Jerusalem stands two thousand feet above sea level and has snow in winter; the valley is one thousand feet below and is hot even in winter; yet these two are but thirty miles apart as the bird flies. Conceived in humour perhaps, and finished with spite, for more than a suggestion of torment has been added to it—as an artist might give a finishing touch to his picture. It would seem that what God commenced the Devil completed.

No sound disturbs the natural stillness; all is quiet with an eerie depressing stillness that is maddening. Sound echoes and re-echoes, a shot fired on one side is audible on the other with almost magnified intensity.

Flies and mosquitoes carry their germ-infected bodies to beast and man, tainting everything, distributing disease everywhere, annoying all as they cluster and fasten to us. Despite all the venom heaped into this place, it seems as if the Maker or perhaps better, the Finisher, could not remain satisfied and charged the atmosphere to permeate even into our minds.

Scientists have said that habitation here in summer is impossible for white men, yet this is what we are essaying to do. Even the natives, hardened to it all as they are through generations, sneak away to avoid the heat of summer.

In the early morning the thermometer rushes quickly up to the hundred mark then slowly creeps higher and higher as the day wears on. Usually it stops at one hundred and twenty but quite often, feeling particularly spiteful, will continue climbing even to one hundred and thirty. One hundred and thirty degrees of enervating heat that makes our blood run hot and our heads go sick. No need to await death to enter hell, it is here on earth.

The malaria scourge has become so great that we struggle to decrease the mosquito pest, which is filling the hospitals to overflowing. Weeks of back-breaking toil in the gruelling heat, many dropping as the fever grips them whilst they work. All these little winding *wadis* provide innumerable backwashes of still water, havens for the mosquitoes to hatch and breed their germs. All have to be straightened out so that there is no stationary water to provide breeding grounds, hundreds of little streams with thousands of little backwashes.

Weeks we spend doing this by day, and supplying outposts by night, never relaxing our vigilance. It is double work and as men go out each day with the fever those who stay find duties constantly increasing. . . .

* * * * * * * *

Yesterday two sections of our troop came over to the Jordan bridgehead for guard duty. We count ourselves extremely fortunate, as when not on shift we can cool at our leisure in the river; we don't care how long the war lasts now, here is ease and a little comfort.

At sunset yesterday afternoon a food convoy passed over the bridge accompanied by the inevitable dust clouds which acted as a marker to the Turkish artillery who immediately opened fire, using composite shells. These are nasty missiles, they explode overhead with shrapnel then continue on again to detonate on contact.

I had been quietly reading in the shade of a bivouac sheet, engrossed by a book of verse I always carried, when the first shells came over. They exploded so near that the vicious swish of the flying pellets was distinctly audible, some falling at my feet.

We had no funk holes or other protection, so we scattered quickly seeking what shelter we could. I crawled under a corduroy culvert in the roadway, built so low to the ground that once in I could scarcely move, much less turn over. The pitter-pat of the falling pellets on the wooden planks overhead so close to my back gave me quite a prickly sensation. Hundreds and hundreds of them fell, enough to kill a goodly number of men, yet those boards were just too thick and provided a very safe haven. I shall use it again today, for the convoy passes each afternoon. Smith was sitting on the railing of the bridge when the first burst occurred. A flying splinter caught his rifle, so surprising him that he overbalanced and fell back into the river. The shelling lasted for fully half an hour, by which time I was badly cramped in my burrow and pleased when released to stretch my limbs. Our camp presented a sorry sight, nearly everything we possessed was riddled, including my precious volume of verse.

Last night we caught a spy, right on the bridge. He was a German dressed as a native. We asked him questions he could not answer, so we held him for the Intelligence who took him away this morning. We don't know where, or care much.

* * * * * * * *

An issue of medals has just taken place. (We always say 'issue,' for it is more descriptive of the method of bestowal.) When something meritorious is done by a group of men, the senior receives the award; that is why nearly all officers and few privates have medals. Of course we realise that everyone could not be honoured. Occasionally a ranker may do something conspicuous and be personally recommended, but that does not often happen. Usually a regiment is notified that so many decorations are available, it being left to the Commanding Officer to pass them on. This is why we say they come in bully beef tins, just like rations to be issued out.

One of our sergeants today received a foreign decoration. He has done nothing to earn it, but he is very popular and we are glad he has it. We tormented him and asked to know how he wangled it, so that we can all have medals too. He admits that he has done nothing to merit it, but says it will please his old folks at home. He laughs at this, thinking it a good joke, and we laugh too, for we like him and he does not mind our humour. It is good to give these medals away, even if some are not earned. It is like the knighthoods at home—the effect is good.

We have been discussing a story of a medical sergeant in a base hospital who has never heard a shot fired. He has an enviable soft job with plenty to eat, a nice uniform to wear and plenty of leave to wear it. He lives in comfort and does his work well. He was always present when brass hats were about and earned their approval by his constant presence, so they gave him a D.C.M. In the orders of the day it is cited as having been awarded for devotion to duty.

* * * * * * * *

The natural formation of the valley with its flat floor, hemmed in and overlooked by the foothills on either side, required much vigilance. The Turk holds all one side of the valley and part of the other; we have the remainder and the river bed. It is easy for him to shell us from his elevation, but to attack he must pass across the flat expanse of the valley. Because of this our line is partly trenched, and partly a series of consolidated positions. This formation and method of defence requires countless patrols and reconnaissances.

One morning we leave on a patrol which will occupy all day; it is not known if our objective is manned or not. If it is we hope

JERICHO

SAND-CART AMBULANCES AND DESERT DRESSING STATION

to draw fire so that our guns can estimate the distance and reply. If not we will scout around the position and gain what knowledge we can. It is not pleasant, this riding as a target to draw fire. As we near the hills we talk less, each of us intently watching for signs of life, not without trepidation in our hearts.

The position is manned, for about midday the Turk, thinking we have come far enough, opens on us. His fire drawn, our task is finished. We gallop back, sustaining few casualties, for it is not easy to hit a quickly moving target unless numerous guns are employed to do it. We have numbers of these patrols, and sometimes are not fired on at all. Another day we make a demonstration in strength. The Turk opens all his artillery, to which ours replies. We cannot return immediately, for the fire is too heavy. Dismounting, we skirmish on foot, holding a position till darkness falls to shelter our return.

Days roll by, each a little more deadly and monotonous than the last. We are gradually reaching a stage where we care little about anything, whether we live or die. Privation and sickness have us half dead now. We continue to provide the patrols, but they are becoming more and more difficult as our bodies weaken with fever.

Word comes one day of another attempt to scale the plateau. After our previous disastrous affair up there we are not very exhilarated by the suggestion. Our bodies are so weak, and our minds so burdened, that we no longer see things in their true perspective. The proposed assault provides two reasons to achieve greater willingness in us than if we had not been there before. We shall be able to escape this murderous valley for a little, with all its heat and disease. That we leave it for conditions of greater hazard is of little consequence, we are unable properly to appreciate how great that hazard is, our minds have become so warped with this incessant heat and no respite. We care little for what awaits us, conditions cannot be worse than here; the heat, we know, will be less. The possibility of death concerns us little, it is much easier to die by a bullet than by the fever and heat which rot us here.

The other reason of our willingness, and by no means the lesser, is that of a score to be repaid. All of us have dear friends up there, whose bodies lie we know not where. We have not forgotten them, nor have we forgotten that it was there we suffered defeat, and to us defeat is intolerable. Because of these things we find a willingness to venture which is more apparent than usually is when we go forth. We will make this attempt with a cause, and if we fail it will not be our fault any more than was the disaster which overtook us on the first attempt.

* * * * * * * *

Again we use the goat paths to ascend, but the other side of the roadway from the previous endeavour. It is hoped that, having scaled the heights, we can attack from above in concert with the infantry below and so force the roadway, thus dividing the Turkish army in two.

The weather is more favourable to us on this venture, but the Turk far more hostile. We have to fight our way up, the Turk contesting every foot of the way, but do so with remarkably few casualties, in marked contrast to the losses suffered by the enemy. Finally bursting through we take the village, our objective. In doing this we have isolated ourselves completely from all land communication with the forces below. We are now entirely dependent on ourselves for our very existence. The Turk holds us like an octopus and is determined to retain his grip; still I think he will not find that easy; we will be difficult to digest.

The village ours, we turn to the roadway and concentrate all our strength towards its capture. This proves more arduous than anticipated and, to increase our handicap, the infantry cannot gain a purchase in the foothills below.

In a few days the failure of the plan is obvious. Looking to ourselves we find the position has become extremely hazardous, and our complete isolation is the more dangerous in that our food is almost exhausted. The supplies we carried for man and beast were for a few days only; had the infantry broken through we would replenish by medium of the roadway. We tooth-comb the village and eat what little we find, mostly native pancakes made of flour and water cooked by heat only and without fat of any kind. Ordinarily they would be repulsive but now we find them quite palatable.

The village lies in a depression completely surrounded by hills, which we have manned since our entry. The horses are picketed below in the village; we hear their neighings as hunger grips them. Though we have the same pains as they we are far more concerned for them than for ourselves. Little or no grass grows amongst the boulder-strewn hill sides, so we cannot graze them.

We have not been able to bring artillery into these hills, as was to have been accomplished when the roadway fell. Deprived of this necessary arm, we make shift with machine-guns and our rifles and grenades. Planes fly over daily and drop quantities of bombs on the Turks. These have to suffice in lieu of shells but, though devastating in effect, they have not the value of concentrated fire definitely directed. We cannot use these bombs as a barrage to attack with. Each night sees fighting of some degree along our scattered line. Mostly it is initiated by the Turk, but one night we go over and carry the war to his side.

* * * * * * * *

I do not know whether we advanced by arrangement or whether the Turk forestalled us and we moved to repel him. We were lying below the crest of a ridge quietly awaiting whatever was to come, when suddenly all was thunder and fire. It happens all so quickly that we are amongst it without knowing if we have been ordered.

Turkish figures quickly appear ahead as their artillery barks and sends the shells bursting amongst us. We lie along the ground pumping our rifles and guns, whilst inwardly our hearts thump. The old fears possess us, the familiar shrieks and shouts echo about. The night, which a few minutes before had been deadly calm, is now a howling bedlam with all the allied noises of licensed slaughter let loose. In a few minutes, from quietly expectant, half nervous soldiery, we become howling lunatics whose only apparent ambition seems to be the slaughter and devastation of the earth's fairest flower, that divine creation, Humanity.

I find myself sheltering in a hollow and not very clear what it is all about, but I don't worry about that. My only thought is to come to the journey's end, whatever that may be or whatever it may bring, to get there as soon as possible. Whispering voices attract my attention, and peering into the dark I find four others in the hollow. I do not recognise them; their faces are strange, but that is nothing so long as they are our own. One is groaning, having been dragged to this shelter by a second. My attention is attracted by a figure directly approaching us. The headgear seems Turkish but it is too dark for me to be sure. Peering intently I see the rifle. Yes, it is a Turk; that rifle is longer than ours. Raising my own weapon I follow his movements as he draws near; he has something in his hand; a grenade; fearing he may see us and fling it, I carefully aim and fire. A gurgle follows the shot, nothing more, and another soul is plunged into hell or heaven.

The vortex swings towards our hollow. Swamped by the seething tide, we think of nothing but loading and firing. It produces in me that frenzy which makes decent men find joy in the killing of their fellow humans. Creating a lust prompted by the one idea, to get it over, to kill or be killed. Many battles had overcome in me the natural revolt and nausea of all this slaughter. To some it comes naturally, to others it is environment, to all a necessity. It has to be, for it is War.

The fighting swings away again, leaving one of my companions dead. Of the other three, one was wounded when he came here, the other two crawl back with him and leave me in sole possession of the hollow. I lie watching and waiting, watching that I am not surprised, waiting for God only knows what. A party of Turks move by, miss my hole, and are swallowed up in the darkness. Rising up on my elbow I look round, but can see nothing, only hear.

A stretcher-party passes, I can just make them out. Their direction puzzles me, either they are moving obliquely or else are not sure of their way; in either case it leaves me doubtful as to my position. I am some hundreds of yards from where we originally set out, unless we came at an angle. I am not sure about this, the first minutes in the beginning are so hazy.

Remaining here I am liable to become isolated; the inactivity, too, irks me. Creeping out on hands and knees I follow the track of the stretcher-bearers, stumbling over a body before I had gone more than a few yards. Rising to my feet a whistling like hornets sends me headlong to the ground as a machine-gun burst passes. Crawling again I find the ground sloping away, and this gives me some idea of my position. I had seen by daylight that this slope ran towards the Turkish lines. By working back in a general direction I hoped to make contact with our own again.

Soon I see a party moving ahead, and as I come up to them some one in charge tells me to join in. They move with caution, so I ask no questions. We have not gone far when a halt is called, and two figures disappear ahead, whilst we remain lying on the ground. In a whisper I ask the man nearest me what it is all about. He is not sure but says a number of these parties are out; he thinks the idea is to work behind the Turkish flank. I then see for the first time that they have a Hotchkiss.

A figure appears ahead and beckons us on; we seem to be moving in a circle. Another party looms up, stationary as if awaiting us to make contact; we all move on together, shortly to encounter a rise in the ground. This we move round and then work up its side. Nearing the top we fall to the ground and crawl ahead till we top the rise; our combined parties then spread out along the ridge top and wait.

A flare goes up and hangs suspended by its little parachute, bathing the surrounding country in light. We slightly overlook a short undulation across which a large body of Turks are moving. The light dies, and as yet nothing has happened though we know what to expect. Another flare passes over, it has no parachute but burns long enough to let us see how near the enemy is to us.

Its light is no sooner gone than a machine-gun crackles into action, followed by others along the line throwing us all into action. Rushing forward we drop and fire as forms emerge from the darkness and take shape. The action swings round; the Turks have evidently engaged the farther end of the line far more than this. Stumbling over a rock I crawl behind it, grateful for the shelter; other figures come up beside me. A break in the night sky enables us to see better.

We pump bullets as fast as we can load. The atmosphere is tense, we strain under our several emotions, nerves keyed to breaking point. The harder the fighting, the greater our tension. My tongue is dry; I wonder what all this effort will avail in the end. I use my rifle in an abandoned delight, finding a savage joy in what little devastation I wreak. It brings me no sorrow to use it club fashion when a too venturesome Turk comes within my reach. I feel no horror as his head cracks under the blow; only an urge which sends me seeking other heads to crack.

A cry near me, I turn and see a battered head where a bullet has found rest, a far too common sight to take notice of unless as perchance now happens. His mate nearby, probably spattered by the blood, rises to his feet; I am close and can see the contortions of his face as he draws himself up. Stretching out his arms he cries to Christ in heaven, then cursing the bloody swine, runs shrieking down the hill with rifle extended and bayonet fixed, rushing to his fate whilst the Devil stands gloatingly by and gathers in another life. A brain stretched till it would stretch no more, but wanted just this to burst the last grip upon his sanity. War makes men beasts, it makes weak men strong, it makes sane men mad; and the Devil stands by and reaps.

As the firing lessens I find myself unconsciously conforming to a general swinging movement so that we face the opposite direction. Rifle-fire and a few desultory machine-gun bursts still split the night but the sounds are quietening. The night is wearing on, giving way to the oncoming light which slowly is diffusing the sky.

As the first rays of light appear we crawl back to our original line of the night before, from where we can see across the terrain ahead. Sunrises can be very hideous when the Devil walks abroad.

****

We have food for neither man nor horse. This is nothing new or unusual, for we have often been dependent on the country and know how to live on it when there is anything to live on. Many times we have taken food from the natives, scoured amongst captured dumps, looted stray sheep or goats. Here, isolated as we are and hemmed in on every side, there is no country to live on. We have managed a few native pancakes but they are not very palatable, tasting like the natives smell. The few cattle in the village have been commandeered and shared amongst us but still we hunger. . . .

I had been oiling my rifle, filling an idle moment, more to provide occupation than because the rifle needed attention. As I sat, Smith came struggling up the hill, a bundle under his arm. Unwrapping it, there lay revealed to our delighted gaze a huge steak. No one bothered to ask how he came by this, we were more concerned about devouring it. A few minutes and a fire was blazing, then soon a tantalising odour as we sniffed the cooking meat. Smith sat with an intense expression on his face, now and then prodding the meat and feeding the fire so that the cookery be the more hurried. We could not wait till it was fully done but must snatch it off and take our share as soon as the rawness was gone.

At the first bite and as the taste circulated I looked at Smith and remarked that it was a nice piece of cow and asked him where he had obtained it.

'Oh down the village, they found some more this morning.'

'Funny that only you seem to know about it. Peculiar tasting cow too, sure it isn't horse? Seems a bit coarse.'

'It is horse,' he replied, 'some were killed last night and I happened to know about it and there you are.'

Still what did it matter? We've eaten camel and goat before today, and other food far less clean too.

Later in the afternoon some of our planes flew over and, swooping low down, dropped a number of tins of biscuits. The impact broke them a little, but that mattered nothing, they nevertheless remained food. It is a big task to feed over a division of men by plane; we do not get much each, but still it is something. Smith's steak had appeased our hunger for the time; he is very handy at foraging. Since I left the gun we have been together in the same section. I have lost interest in the little Hotchkiss after Banks and Miles had gone, for the new men who came in their place were not the same, and I preferred being in the troop with others I liked better. . . .

****

It seems if for a second time we must vacate these hills. We are not sorry to be free of them but we still irk under an undischarged promise to dead comrades, aggravated more now in that this is the second time we have been forced out. If only the infantry could have broken through the roadway! Still, another time will come and perhaps then we will be more successful; but we bitterly resent this backing out, savouring as it does too much of defeat.

Preparations go on for our last night here. Outposts are placed, the usual routine is continued, we act in the line as if retreat was our last thought, firing endless shots just to help the delusion.

By the goat paths we came up and by them we must return. This means that only those able to sit a horse will get out. Our dead have been buried but the lot of the wounded is an unhappy one. We have no wheeled transport, no means whatever of getting men out who cannot ride a horse or walk on foot; these hills are far too treacherously precipitous. It is as much as we sound and healthy ones can do; for wounded it would be impossible. It is decided that those who cannot be carried out must remain behind, dependent on Turkish chivalry. It is terrible that these unfortunates who have given their all should now be deserted and left to an enemy's mercy; it is very sad, but it is also War.

To our regiment falls the rearguard, an unenviable task, for the chances of our escape intact are very remote. The main column creeps out under shelter of darkness, taking with them as many wounded as they can. Broken men bear up under excruciating agonies, sticking it out, riding in front of their mates whilst others lead their horses. We who remain scatter out along a ridge previously held by ten times our number and keep up a semblance of undiminished strength. Firing endless cartridges at nothing, we strive to make the sounds of night seem as usual. To withdraw the advance outposts necessitates that men must pass through our line to warn them; it is dark and as they return we challenge them. Trigger-fingers are nervous, for the fate of a division depends on us. One returning man crawling up to the line does not hear the challenge and moves forward, even after a second warning, to receive a bullet.

As the tail of the column disappears word comes to be ready for the evacuation. When all is complete runners come up the slope and warn us. On receiving the word we rush down the hill, mount our horses and quietly but quickly move into the night. Haste is essential for we know the Turk will become in-quisitive when the firing ceases and will seek to know why. Scouts will soon elucidate this, and pursuit would be bad for us along these narrow tracks.

As the last of our column passes through the village, some of the inhabitants, realising the significance of all this movement, display their antagonism to us by rifle fire. We fling a few gre-nades into the houses we pass, to pay for their treachery. This display alarms us for the safety of our wounded left behind. We have ho time to retaliate as these ingrates deserve but if we should come again, we will repay; we do not forget such things, which perhaps is one reason why we are regarded as such im-placable troops, and in part has earned for us the reputation of a remorseless enemy. We forget neither good nor bad.

It was well after midnight when we left with a ride of some hours ahead of us, made the more difficult by lead horses and the wounded we carry. As the morning light grows in brilliance we come under fire; it has not taken the Turk long to discover our escape. He believed us securely held, and knowing that he could not take us by force of arms, he probably hoped to starve us out; but he reckoned without due consideration of the men he opposed.

It is not long before artillery is brought to bear on us. This complicates our journey for we cannot stay to seek cover, but must keep constantly moving, and chance the added risk exposure brings. We slither as best we can down the tortuous and narrow paths, the twisting of which had before brought curses to our lips but for which we are now grateful as the twists and turns provide some cover. A few are unfortunately wounded as we move, but are quickly hoisted up, irrespective of their wounds, and journey on.

Emerging into the valley, we each receive some biscuits from a dump laid down for this special purpose only a few hours before. We eat them ravenously and are thankful. This food reminds me of some native pancake I have, and taking it from my wallets I try to eat but find the taste too repulsive. Yesterday it was good food, but after just a few civilised biscuits it sickens my stomach. Surprising what the human stomach accepts as good when hunger commands.

CHAPTER 8

Life in the Valley

How still the air is! Not a breath of movement! The heat goes rippling over the valley in waves, withering our bodies and the souls within. Heavy toll we have paid to occupy this fiendish place but heavier yet must we pay. Our ranks are continuously thinning, and few of our regiment who originally entered this valley now remain. Those who escaped death and injury on the plateau are falling before his unavoidable fever scourge.

Our troop is nearly all new faces, but a few of the old familiars remain. Cox, sitting over there fixing his saddle, still goes on and Lenny too. They are tough these twain, it would take an axe to kill them. I can hear Lenny arguing with Smith in our bivouac nearby. Smith has the fever and will not eat; I am worried about him; it will only be a few days and he will be gone. He fights so hard against it, is determined to throw it off. But it is no use: one morning he will ride away in the ambulance; I dread to think of that; we have been together so long and escaped so much together. Others move about, mostly new arrivals; they will not last long, they never do, a week perhaps or maybe two. They are not acclimatised as we are. They come, are of service for a handful of seconds (as Smith expresses it), and then are gone. It must be the lives they have lived which enables these old hands to keep going. Born and bred in the Bush, reared and inured to hardship, strangers to comfort and luxury. Old soldiers all of them, with years of service to reconcile them to the heat. How I keep going myself I do not know, unless it is by the healthy life I have always led.

Each week sees new men arriving, but always only a few, never enough to fill our ranks. Some are old hands who have been away wounded or sick, others dug out of base jobs because of the acute shortage of man power, or, to quote Smith again, cannon fodder. Many of them are getting their first taste of war. Whichever it be, they all, or nearly all, go the same way. It is impossible to come here in the height of summer and survive. We who still manage to hang on came in before the heat was at its zenith and have been able to adjust ourselves to it with the foundation of much past campaigning. These new arrivals come along, soldier for a few days, or perhaps weeks, but only as long as it suits the valley. One day, Old Man Jordan, thinking they have stayed long enough, stretches out his all-enveloping mantle and carries them off.

Gunshot wounds take their toll, but mostly it is the malaria; many would willingly have wounds in exchange for this cursed fever. It brings about a see-sawing temperature. One minute its victims are sweating with heat, the next rolled shivering in blankets, shivering when the shade temperature is one hundred and twenty or more. Often the blood turns jet black, they cannot eat, just lie in the shade doing nothing but drink huge quantities of water. It is not possible for everyone developing fever to be removed, as this would mean the line becoming deserted; only the very bad cases go out. The others hang on, some get worse and go away, others recover and take their accustomed place in the line again. Occasionally variation is provided by someone going off his head, to be carried away raving. Usually they recover, but a few probably never will, the canker of the valley biting too deeply into their brains.

Is it any wonder that men go this way? Mentally we are all dulled, the heat clouds our faculties so that they function spasmodically. The food too is insufficient and bad; we are only half nourished. It is not the powers' fault this; they do what they can for us; it is our location right up here that makes transport so difficult.

113

Our diet has little variation, mostly bully beef and mildewed bread with onions, sometimes a tin of jam as a luxury. The heat turns the beef-fat into oil. We place the tins in *wadi* beds to cool but the water is half-tepid, so it is not much use. Usually when we prod a tin with the bayonet preparatory to opening, the liquid fat squirts out.

The bread is made a long way off, and comes to us in sacks as large as chaff bags, always broken, seldom more than a few whole loaves in each sack, dried and hard with mould penetrating right through. We have long been used to this mould and scarcely notice it; hunger has overcome any squeamishness we may have once had; the bread is too precious to waste by scraping the green away. Day in, day out, diet is the same, and our stomachs revolt against so much repetition but there is nothing else unless it be an occasional tin of mixed vegetable and meat. This makes us rejoice and we treat it with well merited honour. We have ways of disguising the inevitable bully. Mixing it with bread or, when we have it, flour, frying the lot and calling the result rissoles. The flour is never enough to make a damper, but enough to provide a cloak for the constant bully so that we may think it something else and hope to deceive our stomachs thereby.

The great consolation is that tea, our mainstay, is regular. Without this we would indeed be lost; it helps keep our thirst down and is very comforting in many ways. When we have jam we only get what it suits the flies to leave for us. When a tin is opened they swarm over the surface and though we beat the air about the opening tin, they nevertheless get in, swarming over the surface and completely coating it. As quickly as we remove them others take their place. As we spread the jam on bread, they swarm around so that it is impossible to avoid eating them too or else lose the food. What does it matter anyway, we are not epicures that we should grumble; some say that our meat supply is thereby increased; at least it's the only fresh meat we get.

At a small canteen at Jericho various tinned foods are obtainable. Whenever anyone goes there they always bring back what they can carry. Without this service we would not exist at all, the army ration would surely finish us.

Smith was removed this morning; he went off his head during the night. He put up a good struggle, too good—he must pay for his courage. How thin he has grown, his ribs sticking out like xylophone keys, one could almost strike matches on them! I will miss his cheery face, his ever-ready wit, but above all his wonderful comradeship. I shall never forget his worn and emaciated appearance, tribute to the great-hearted soldier he always was. His indomitable courage and determination to stick it through have claimed payment for his fortitude. Never virtuous or troubled about his morals, sincere in what he did for others, a hard liver, but above all a man. His loss to me is the greatest personal calamity of the campaign. I loved him.

* * * * * * * *

I have had a septic leg for some weeks past; today on removing the bandage, to my joy I see it healed. On outpost one night I badly scratched myself crawling through some gorse bushes and as always happens, sepsis set in.

Each day I went to the doctor, who scraped away the putrefying flesh with a scalpel. It is a painful process and naturally no one likes it, but as we all have these sores we take it as a matter of course. It is impossible to avoid them; the air is impregnated with the sepsis which penetrates the slightest break in the skin.

Many have their own cures to avoid the doctors, chiefly water purification tablets, a barbarous though popular method and of doubtful efficacy. I tried this way but the tablets only effervesced in the wounds, stung a lot and did not help. I asked that I might be allowed to use boracic, but was forbidden and told that the method employed was the only successful one. Determined to try my own way of drying up the sores, I asked Lenny to get the boracic for me. He told the medical orderly it was for his eyes; as we often suffer from the glare his excuse was reasonable. My leg had become so sensitively tender from constant cutting that I was willing to try anything to avoid the scalpel.

The day after applying the boracic we went out on a stunt for a week which forbade any attention to my sores. We never had our clothes off so that I had of necessity to await return to camp before seeing if my cure was good or not. Unlacing my trousers I had to pull them forcibly from the bandage through which the festering had seeped sticking both together like glue. It was with great difficulty and many grunts and curses that I eventually removed the matted bandage to find my leg looking worse than before. Still having a little boracic left I powdered it on, wishful still to persevere with my own method. A few days later, when again the bandage was removed, to my delight the sores were drying and now today the leg is well again but I will not be telling the doctor.

Everybody seems to be contaminated by the sepsis, particularly the hands, as we knock them in the course of our duties. It is impossible to avoid these running sores; if we do not get them from knocks it is from scratching the flesh raw when the lice bite.

* * * * * * * *

Today with Lenny I went into Jericho with lead horses for reinforcements coming to our regiment. They are becoming very scarce these days, available men are getting fewer and fewer.

We rode all the morning through the blinding dust and grilling heat, not so annoying to us now as we think of the canteen awaiting our pleasure at Jericho. Elated at the thought of some decent food we hurried our trip and with pleasurable anticipation entered the tent where it was to be had and bought a tin of fruit and one of salmon. Finding a shady spot we opened the cans and soon gorged ourselves to repletion. Gorged indeed! For soon we were grovelling in the dust as pains went shooting through our bellies. Seeing the Red Cross over a tent nearby we hurried across, thinking perhaps the food was tainted. A medical sergeant gave us some medicine and told us that it served us right for being so gluttonous; coming down from the valley where our food was so different we had been very unwise to fill ourselves with food far too rich for our maltreated stomachs. We had not thought of this, had hardly realised that such could happen; but apparently it is common, for the sergeant says men from the line often come to him with the same complaint.

Sitting outside the tent a poor devil of a Tommy infantryman was brought in under escort, he had shot himself through the calf of his leg but omitted to place a bag over the limb first, and the powder had burned his trousers, offering irrefutable evidence of self-infliction. He would be healed, then sent away for court-martial and sentenced for self-inflicting a wound. The sergeant told us that he had had a number of these fellows through his hands. It is not surprising, it is more to be wondered at that more suicides do not happen; the valley is sufficient to weaken the strongest minds. Riding back during the afternoon heat, Lenny amused himself by painting as black a picture as he could of the valley. He derived amusement from the evident discomfiture of new men already ruing the fate that had brought them here. When he thought he had said enough he justified himself to me by explaining that it was better they should find the valley less deadly than he had told than worse.

Any distractions we have from the monotony of our daily routine are provided by ourselves, there are no rest huts or concert parties here, nor is it possible that any such form of entertainment could be provided. Our amusement devolving on us as it does, takes what to the uninitiated may seem an extraordinary form, but to us is as logical as a cricket match would be at home.

Our favourite pastime is baiting spiders or scorpions. We catch these insects during the day and when the sun has set, but before darkness, set them upon each other. It is common to see men congregated in groups around a biscuit tin in which are the contestants, men absorbed as if a great deal were at stake, and in fact a great deal often is, for very large bets are made and lost on the sting of a scorpion or the bite of a spider.

When all bets have been laid the spiders or scorpions, sometimes it is one of each or perhaps two spiders or scorpions, are placed in the tin, which is shaken to enrage the combatants then placed so as to permit as many as possible obtaining a view of the proceedings. As soon as the tin is still the fighters will attack each other with deadly venom; they give no quarter, struggling till one is dead, sometimes killing each other. Seemingly a callous amusement, but nevertheless one peculiarly suited to our circumstances. We have a special dislike for these creatures; their bite is poisonous and extremely painful, as most of us have discovered at some time. We never worry what the contestants are, spider or scorpion. Some of these little fellows achieve fame by killing all that are opposed to them and become the centre of greater attraction, so that betting then is at odds. This will happen with a number who will rise in prowess above their fellows, so that eventually an extra special match is arranged on which wagers of really surprising amounts are placed. Interest is correspondingly great; many a prize-fighter would rest satisfied with as much.

These creatures are not ordinary specimens as are found at home, but a breed of giants. Scorpions grow in some cases to the length of a pencil whilst the spiders are no less; many would overlap a saucer. They fight with deadly hatred, and are so venomously tenacious in their methods that it is common for them to become locked together to the undoing of both.

* * * * * * * *

For a week past I have been possessed of an increasing lethargy. It has gradually fastened itself on me, so that everything requires an effort. My head spins and reels when I move, outposts are a curse; I find contentment only in idleness, which creates a peaceful lassitude. Watering the horses requires great effort to keep the saddle, often I dismount and hold the stirrup leather to support myself, otherwise I would fall off.

I know what it is and strive to fight it off; yet I know it is useless; we all succumb to it in the end. Everything is so impregnated with fever that to struggle is hopeless. So many splendid examples of grit and determination are daily seen that it becomes natural to hang on as long as possible, for though eventually we must give in we are still of use till we do, and make the load of our fellows a little lighter. Our numerical strength is so low that every man is badly needed, too badly needed to give way easily. Stricken with malaria or any of its kindred ailments, forced to keep going, unable to receive attention, one gets beyond conscious effort, but acts just as a sleep-walker would do. A task is accomplished by throwing the mind forward to the ease to come when it is finished, by keeping one's thoughts away from the present misery and looking to the anticipated rest.

We have developed a sort of pride which forces us on; we know the homelands are being bled of men and the demand cannot be fully met. Many of course shirk behind an excuse to better themselves in our absence, but they are a type that we would sooner remain at home: we do not want them here. Every man is so badly needed, the depleted strength of each unit daily becomes more and more apparent, that we hang on and strive, forcing our bodies through agony. A few of softer material give in, earning the contempt of their fellows, but that is not very often.

Generally they too hold up, wishful to follow the example of others made of tougher stuff, and in the end pay the more dearly for doing so. These earn our great respect, for we value our reputation, and those who help build it are men to be esteemed, whilst those who weaken are despised till a day comes when they can creep away and never come back. They may go to easy base jobs but there no call is made on their courage so they can do us no harm.

One's perspective when gripped with the fever is liable to become distorted, so that the ultimate end is of no account and a bullet considered a welcome relief. It is then that the danger of collapse is so great. It has happened that some poor devil not mentally strong enough to fight against the lurking suggestion in his brain, or even perhaps deranged by the very effort of fighting against it, has taken this way out. If he kills himself it is no matter. If it is a wound he is healed, then tried before a court whose members have never known the mental stress that the poor unfortunate has passed through. They will put him in gaol for a few months with hard labour. Temporary aberration is something they may have entirely failed to consider.

I have come to the stage when my legs will no longer function; if I haul myself upright I can only stagger a few paces and then fall. Crawling into my bivouac I collapse, and stay there doing nothing but drink. Days go by and I eat nothing; I have tried but only vomit it, so that now even the thought of food turns my stomach. Daily I drink gallons of water; I do not know whether I should do this and don't care. Each morning one of the fellows fills my two canvas water buckets and each night they are empty again. I sweat the water out as fast as it is drunk, yet despite this the shivers constantly claim me so that I roll beneath all the blankets I can find though the temperature is so high.

On the seventh day I stagger a few yards and eat my first food, some papped biscuit. A few days more and again I ride with the horses to water. I am still wretched and sick and have weak moments when it would be very easy to give in. I conquer them, for many others have stuck it out and there is no reason why I should not; it is only what countless others have done and what we all expect of each other. It has become so common to see men struggle thus that it is scarcely noticed. Only in the exceptional case, where a weakling fights as a giant, do we stop to watch the struggle and feel admiration for his courage.

* * * * * * * *

Days drag by, each one increasing our despair just a little more. Hardly anyone that has not had the fever, some two and three times. Duties are becoming increasingly difficult, outposts are more common for there are fewer of us to do them. Trenches and redoubts must be dug, iron stakes driven into the ground, yards upon countless yards of barbed wire twisted around them.

Some of this work is done at night, under the sheltering arm of darkness, but much must of necessity be done by day under the blazing sun, which is sweating us into walking skeletons. We are constantly in the thick and hot knee-breeches now, instead of the shorts we once used; a new parasite has been discovered which attacks the human knee if uncovered. This makes labour more fatiguing, as we work away digging interminable trenches and fortifying them to withstand attack, consolidating our positions for battles to come.

Nearly every day the Turk opens his artillery as we dig. It is not always possible to get beneath the ground for shelter, so we drop where we are on the sun-baked surface. The contact burns us, especially if the ground is flinty or gravelly, and then we blister.

We are finding out what a vindictively hopeless place this valley is as it entangles us all. Disease or poisonous bites get everyone; if we escape the one there is always the other and the little adders, too, whose bite is death, as has happened to many. If we withstand the pestilences it gets our souls, rots them with an ever-increasing mental canker. We are ceasing to be normal, too long have we grilled on the hobs of hell. To think too much brings despair and in its train the realisation of the utter hopelessness of the place. Bullets and shells are the least of the troubles. We do not worry so much about them; they have taken second place to the awful conditions under which we exist. Numbers go out each day through wounds, but far more through disease. The less thought given to our condition the better; it is wiser for the brain to remain somnolent. Too much thought provides food for the mental canker always ready to beset those who will let it. Even our bodies are not the same. I cut my finger opening a tin. The blood trickles forth like ink, a thin black substance that once was rich and red. Perhaps I dwell too much on this, but at present my mind is occupied by a sight I saw this morning. A man tied to the bottom of a limber to restrain his struggles. His shrieks and piercing cries still echo in my ears; he thought he was being murdered, poor devil. He had let the valley enter his brain and so had toppled into the deep, dark, ever-waiting abyss.

CHAPTER 9

Out of the Line

The sun does not seem so hot today. Really it is, but my heart is singing. A few leave passes have been granted, one to my squadron and I am next due. Ten glorious days completely to myself, to do with as I wish, and when and how I wish. No one to order me about, no bad food. I shall be able to sit in comfort and eat what I like and as much and as often as I like, and get drunk too if it suits me. My foot-weariness has passed away; I do not notice so much the tiredness that has beset me for so long past. It is eighteen long months since I last saw Cairo and I would not be seeing it now, only the length of waiting has been cut down by those ahead passing out. No leave has been granted for months, and now it has come only four men from our regiment may go. Three months ago I was nowhere near due, yet in that short time sickness and death have brought me to being the next man eligible. A tinge of sadness accompanies the thought, for through it one realises more how much we have suffered.

At Jericho we clamber into some empty motor-lorries going back to Jerusalem. Ours breaks down, so we do not arrive till late at night. Too late to get out to the details, so we decide to sleep at the station. Enquiring for our train, we find a fairly clean truck and crawl to rest.

Mathews, the man next me, has a piece of dry bread which the lorry driver had given him, which he shares with me. We are hungry but have no money and, except for this bread, no food.

We could not take any from our fellows in the valley but we are not troubled; we would be poor soldiers if we could not forage all we need on the way.

The trip to the plain does not take long, about nine in the morning the train pulls into a siding where it will remain for a few hours. Seeing a Y.M.C.A. flag flying, Mathews and I make towards it, hoping to obtain some food. The minion of benevolence who is in charge cannot at first be found but we wait till he arrives and tell him that we are off on leave, and have no money, but a good appetite. He explains that he can do nothing for us, that he must account for all the foodstuff's he has and if he gave any away he would have to make it up.

Mathews points out that even if this is so it would not impose a big strain on his Christian conscience if he gave a little light weight to balance it. He indignantly remarks that he is above that sort of thing. I tell him that the fellows about here are all communication men who do no fighting, a little short weight from them to us who do, should not burden his conscience; but this argument too is fruitless. As a last resource Mathews suggests that he invite us to breakfast, at least the Y.M.C.A. will not call upon him for an accounting of his own rations. It is useless though, he is very mean for he replies that we may not be genuine front line men but cadgers or lead-swingers. We show him our passes, but, not wishing to be convinced, he again excuses himself.

The injustice of it makes us smart; we feel humiliated too, begging as we were.

Walking away in disgust we encounter a Tommy canteen. Entering, we ask for the sergeant-in-charge and explain the position to him. His only comment is that the Y.M.C.A. never gives anything away it can sell. Turning behind his counter, he presents us with a tin of sausages, some bread and jam and tea. We are really very grateful and cannot thank him enough. He merely smiles, saying to eat it up and forget it. I mentally promise him a bottle of rum on my way back. His generosity is the more appreciable as these canteens are admittedly run for profit by the canteens board. And none the less so as he belongs to a country different from ours and a different arm of the service.

The train eventually decides to get along with its business and after many hours of stopping and starting, intermingled with occasional shunts, we arrive at Gaza of sad memory. Having a little time to spare here Mathews and I decide to look round.

Quite a large cemetery has sprung up, hundreds of graves running in serried rows, in contrast to the hurried burials which long ago marked the committing to earth of our dead. Casualties had been so heavy that large pits were dug, into which the dead were tipped from the limbers in which they were gathered, dumped into these holes like so much rubbish. It was Tommy infantry who chiefly suffered here. Photos had been taken of this burying but afterwards their possession was prohibited and those with Cairo photographers confiscated. The action had been a most disastrous one, and the less known of it the better, which was why photos were forbidden under penalty; it would be bad for England to know of such things. Soldiers, when all is said and done, are only pawns to be used at will, but it does not do to tell the British public that.

From Gaza the train rattled on through the desert, with greater speed now and fewer stops, till finally we arrived at Kantara on the Canal, crossed over the bridge and into another train. Travelling in carriages instead of the open trucks of the desert, we flashed through village after village till finally the outskirts of our Mecca approached. I can think of nothing but food though I know I must go very carefully after the valley fare. I have almost forgotten what decent food is like, or the taste of a quart of cold beer.

Pulling at last into the station we are immediately surrounded and besieged by the innumerable Arabs who cluster like so many flies, demanding the usual something for nothing, wanting to carry our gear for a few piastres reward, fighting with us to gain possession of it. Not till we generously helped them with many boot kickings and not a few punches would they leave us and then only to stand at a distance and abuse us. Contact with the Arab has taught me not a few of their choicer expressions, so they probably received as much, verbally, as they gave, and a good deal more physically.

Outside the station Mathews and I clambered into a *gharri*, telling the driver after we escaped the clamouring natives, to drive us to the National, the favourite hotel of the common herd when on leave. It is the best that the officers have left us, having commandeered the decent ones for themselves and when a press of them are here, even adding that to the list of *out-of-bounds for troops*. Mathews had facetiously suggested that we go to the Y.M.C.A.

* * * * * * * *

Many privates, the colonials in particular, have as much and often more money at their disposal than their officers, for which reason they are able when such is the case to command the greater attention of hotel servants. This naturally is rather belittling to subalterns with a sense of dignity, for no one who considers himself of better clay than the rabble cares to see this rabble receiving greater respect. The fact that it is the rabble's money that commands, and not the person of the rabble, does not mitigate the slight. Further, the subaltern and higher rankers too, but particularly the former, as he is less seasoned and immaturity has not permitted him to realise how empty and useless are the shams which divide society into several *stratum*, resent contact with the common herd, they prefer their atmosphere unpolluted by the lesser orders of humanity. For which reason certain hotels and cafés are for the exclusive use of officers, and no private dare set his foot within the portals of these places, sanctified to the greater glory of superior beings. This system of segregation permits the King's Gentlemen to enjoy all decent hotels to the exclusion of privates who are forced to make do with what is left them. That the leavings are poor in quality is naturally understood, and should be remembered when privates seek occupation in peculiar places, having nothing else to do. We accept this system as a matter of course and though we may smart through it, we nevertheless abide by it and do not complain of it. The average private is to a great extent used to domination by his superiors and takes it as a matter of course. England has for so many centuries divided her peoples into classes, each of which respects and bows down to those above whilst treating with disdain those below. Because of this fragment of feudal overlording inborn through generations, the Tommy finds it far less intolerable than does his colonial cousin. He salutes his officers with respect and never asks why; if he does he is told that it is not the man but the King's commission invested in him that he salutes.

The colonial, coming from a newer and freer country where such abominations and petty uselessness have not penetrated, squirms far more under this domination. That he is debarred from some hotels and must constantly salute is against his democratic principles. In fact a goodly number of his officers have as little time for these petty nothings as the privates themselves and would be as pleased to see their abolition. Amongst the ranks of colonial soldiery are many men who in civil life amount to a good deal more than their present rank indicates and possess more wealth than perhaps may be supposed. In England if one considers himself a gentleman he must have a commission, if he were a private many homes would be closed to him. In the colonies one's rank makes no difference, the majority of our present officers commenced as privates.

This state of affairs gives rise to a rather peculiar position. The Tommy, instead of appreciating the result that democratic colonies are gradually bringing about whereby the Tommy is gaining in that he is slowly becoming less the serf and more the man, resents this incursion into what he considers are the traditions of his country. One would almost believe he preferred to remain an underling, objecting to the social crumbling that is slowly but surely taking place in the walls of a class-bound nation. The colonial is freer and happier, all men are equals and the top of the ladder is available to all, no matter how lowly their birth. The Tommy prefers that the top be reserved for those who by birth are its heirs, prefers that his humble feet should not soil it. The war is breaking down a lot of these barriers and a greater emancipation is in sight, but it is being forced, for England in its insularity and cock-of-the-walk manner is naturally a very conservative country and not appreciative of anything that is new or threatens to alter customs of generations.

Because of these things it is not to be expected that colonials and Tommies could be deep friends. The former is happy-go-lucky, taking life as it comes, with no worries and caring little even to the length of being absolutely casual, irrespective of the occasion. He is sincere in what he does, whether it be killing Turks or getting drunk and he does one equally as well as the other. When he fights he fights and everyone knows about it; if they don't, he tells them, so that he has in some degree earned the reputation of a boaster, but whether this be true or not he has acquitted himself sufficiently well to be able to boast. He is loyal to his friends and sincere in his friendships and worries less about colour lines if the man beneath the colour is to his way of thinking worthy of his friendship. Mentally as well as physically he is a husky, which fact is reflected in his actions making him to some extent boisterous, which is objectionable to the quiet-natured Tommy. That he is boisterous (as is the habit of all new nations) gives him a greater forcefulness, tending to override other people. Out of it all emerges one clear fact, that he is naturally a fighter possessed of great vigour, and having set out to do a task is doing it to the greatest extent of his ability.

These things have all tended to create a jealousy of him, and I believe that the Tommies' quiet dislike of him has its seed in this. He does not mix much with the English Tommy but the case is far different with the Scotch; these two are more akin and more closely attuned. The colonial is what he is because of circumstances. His forbears pioneered a new and unknown country. They are or were English stock but the hardier spirits of that stock. To come into a new country as they did required courage and independence as well as stamina and a great heart. From men such as these have sprung our present selves; we are no more than one or two generations removed from these forbears and our country is still too sparsely populated for us to have become sluggish and citified. Is it to be expected that we can be anything else but what we are?

Despite all this we have a lot of respect for the Tommy and admire the many sterling qualities he possesses. That he is more sedate and does not answer to our rougher humour is but the fault of environment and being isolated away in his little island. All our artillery is English and Scotch and no one could have a greater affection for them than we have. Many a colonial has been made to pay for taking up the cudgels of Tommies in squabbles where the latter were at a disadvantage and has done so cheerfully and satisfied in having helped the weaker.

It is but fitting that colonials and Tommies should pull together but it is often made difficult by English regulations and the attitude of many English officers. The free and easy manner of the colonial is not liked and he is always told that he is undisciplined; there is no need for discipline with him if one knows how to handle him, but in this the English officer generally is sadly incapable. He knows how to give orders but his text books do not help him if they are not carried out. England expects her soldiers to do what they are told, they must not have a personality or individuality of their own, their brains must be dormant, they must be automatons. Because we are naturally independent spirits and capable of thought we are considered undisciplined and I am afraid, to many high hats, anathema; but this does not stop them using us to fight their battles, and when we do we get no credit. Many times we read in English papers that British troops have done so and so when only Australians were concerned. We greatly resent this, not that we are un-British but the term Australian could be used and a little credit given us. The English high command is always willing to push these undisciplined troops into battle but grudges them any commendation that is due and have little to say to their good. This adopted attitude of taking all we have and giving little in return does not help the Tommy and

Australian private to pull together as they might. That we have done and are continuing still to do all that is asked us and doing it well, cannot be gainsaid. The Australian geographically is far removed from all this strife; but the fact that he has little to do with this quarrel of nations has not stopped him helping all he can, and how well may be proved when all is over.

Temperamentally these two nations are wide apart, one coming from the cold and half frozen North, the other from the sunny semi-tropical South. One abutting on the edge of Europe, treading in care for fear of entanglements with other nations though half isolated by the Channel, which insularity has tended to narrow its vision. A country old in history and tradition with a reputation as a nation to be guarded, naturally slow-thinking and careful because of her age and experience. Whilst on the other hand we of the antipodes are far removed from European intrigue and ambition, are young and virile which naturally endows us with a care-free demeanour. We have not the weight of tradition to carry and so can be more easy-going and happy. Because of these things it is not the easy matter of pulling together and fraternising as at first one would expect, as we both are from the same tree, so too is America originally and see how they have drifted. Youth there found the bonds created by an older country too irksome and broke away to struggle on its own, and it does not seem to have floundered for lack of parental guidance. England and Australasia, which includes New Zealand, are the two chief ingredients of the Allied forces on this front and it is because of this that we discuss them, hoping to understand them the better for doing so.

Their attitude towards each other is interesting and worthy of observation. The Englishman from an older country feels superior and regards the Australian with an air of lofty condescension as, too, he is inclined to regard the rest of the world, whereas the colonial is indifferent to this attitude, almost contemptuously so.

The crux of the lukewarmness between colonial and Englishman lies in the fact that the former is too free-and-easy, with insufficient respect for the traditions and greater knowledge of an older nation, whilst the latter regards himself too much as being the salt of the earth. To quote an English authority who has put his finger near the weakness, 'The English gentleman of the middle of last century was privileged to despise the other nations of the world. His contempt was distributed geographically as well as temporally and theologically,' and after all we are not far removed from the middle of last century, and a lot of that period still survives in us. The Englishman is even now a reflection in opinion of that period; he has broadened little in tolerance to other countries. By the same token the Australian is still near the same period and his personality has a tinge of those men who made so famous the roaring forties; so it can be understood that these two countries must be dissimilar in temperament, habits and in almost everything but language. We are a volunteer army whereas England is conscript, and she is because her people do what they are told which has laid the base for her much boasted discipline, carried so far that her soldiers must always obey and never question. Essentially true of English practice but fundamentally wrong for all that, are Tennyson's lines.

Theirs not to reason why,
Theirs but to do and die.

England lost America through her overbearing and intolerable dominance; she is not strengthening the bonds of affection between her present dominions now. Those dominions are coming to the place where they too will soon reason for themselves as did America and a question will rise to be answered. It is wise that England in her growing senility remembers that, though the colonies, I think, will never leave England. But the time has come when they should enter of right into her councils. Especially if they are to support England, they should know the why and wherefore.

CHAPTER 10

Cairo

Ensconced in our hotel, first thoughts were for food, a bath and some decent clothes, of the latter I had plenty in my kit bag, also a spare uniform. Considering it useless to wash and change back to our present louse-infested garments, we decided to eat first, then go out to the kit store. Accordingly we went out to a café, having missed the midday meal here, ordered some eggs and bread. I was taking no chances with my stomach, though I longed to eat everything within reach.

Obtaining my kit bag, I immediately noticed how small it had grown, not being half full, whereas when placed here before going up the line last it had been quite full. Opening it I found that my complete uniform and boots, which had been privately made and were my own property, had disappeared, as had also some photos, my razor and a number of other articles. This was not a new happening, many men complained of their possessions being stolen this way, but it is always useless to seek redress.

We have no place where our chattels can be left other than here; we are strangers in a strange land with whom the civilians do not mix, so we must of necessity deposit them here and risk theft. When I drew the attention of the sergeant-in-charge to what had happened he was most voluble in denying that the bag had been tampered with under his care. It makes one almost envious to think (as some authority has put it 'it takes seven men to keep one man in the line') of the nice soft billets these men have, but somehow I prefer my own little niche. I can still respect my manhood which is more than these lice in base jobs can do.

Mathews desiring to make some enquiries concerning a friend at the citadel, we accordingly went direct there from the kit stores as after sundown we would not be admitted.

Whilst he attended to his affairs I wandered about this old fortress, now converted into a military prison, more to occupy my time than with any desire to observe the sights long since familiar to me.

Attracted by a gang of soldier convicts digging a hole near one of the lower walls, I wandered in this direction. Idly watching them for a few minutes, I turned to the sergeant-in-charge and asked why they dug. He explained they were preparing the grave of a spy who was to be executed at sunrise. As he was speaking, one of the men unearthed an old cannon ball, a relic of the Napoleonic invasion, which the digger remarked would make a good headstone. The grave was essentially rude in construction, just a hole scraped in the gravelly soil to which later would be added quicklime to hasten the decomposition of the poor wretch who this time tomorrow will be occupying it. At the sergeant's suggestion I walked up a hill to a tree near a well, the place of execution or, as the sergeant unnecessarily crudely expressed it, the 'shooting gallery.'

The method employed I learned was to tie the condemned to a chair with his back against the tree. To his chest would be attached a target to ensure the greater accuracy of the firing party lying on sandbags some few yards distant. Examining the tree trunk I discovered a number of bullet holes from past executions; mute testimony of a doubtful system.

Taking a seat on a nearby bench, I could not help thinking just how doubtful this system of capital punishment really is. It seems incompatible with the much boasted British justice and freedom that it should exist to such a degree in a conscript army. We are volunteers, and to us it does not apply, though if it did it would be part of the oath we take, and we would be aware of and agreeable to it as we are here of our own free wills and awake to conditions and penalties. With the Tommies however, who are compelled to serve, it stands to reason that amongst men indiscriminately forced, a number must exist who, though physically fit, are not mentally fit to withstand the strain of modern warfare.

Excluding of course those who commit crimes, the penalty for which under any circumstances must be the extreme, whether that be death or imprisonment according to practice, there must nevertheless be many who have incurred death for offences the circumstances of which have rendered it extremely doubtful in accordance with the precepts of justice whether the death sentence should have been passed. One of the most heinous breaches a soldier can commit is to desert, but the sphere of this charge is so elastic that under its heading can be brought many acts which often to the mind of the accused in no way border upon it; often too desertion, in the strict sense of the word, may not be intended. What in base camps is merely termed *absent without leave*, in the field becomes desertion. Few people have any idea of the great number of offences punishable by death. Some seem almost trivial, but in the eyes of military law, nothing is trivial.

Reverting to the man who admittedly has deserted, it is to be remembered that he is compulsorily a soldier, without voice or choice in the matter. Against all laws of liberty he has been seized, clothed with a uniform and a rifle thrust into his hands and simply told to go and kill Huns. No matter what his own feelings or how mentally he may be constituted he must do as he is told. If he refuses, or goes as far as the line and panic or any of a hundred reactions possess him and he flees, he is a deserter. He will be tried by a court of high officers who have not served as privates in the war and so have never been subjected to the mental torment which has eventually caused this dereliction of duty. And if it so chooses it can condemn him to be shot, for the King's Regulations provide that for misbehaving before the enemy in such a manner as to show cowardice, death may be imposed.

133

Doubtlessly when first framed these regulations were intended for good, providing of course that those with the power to carry them out did so according to the spirit implied. But the army as we know it has become so ramified that too many men of the bullying type have crept in; men who are inclined to interpret the Regulations to the letter thinking they grow in importance that way. It is because of this that the Regulations require much tightening and the death penalty removed from many offences to which it now applies.

A man may leave his post with no ulterior motive or intention to desert; but for doing so is he charged as a deserter, and though he escape the full penalty, the stigma remains. A man can be a deserter in any area known as a war zone, even though he be miles from the actual fighting, and the offence is just the same as if he had been guilty of this action in the very front line.

It is not meet that penalties should be nominal, that of course would be ridiculous and court disaster, for an army is not a thing of glass to be handled as a fragile vessel; nor is it the fragrant bloom in an orchard, exuding perfumes for the birds to sing of. An army stinks, it fights, it marches, and it slays or is slain. It is not wise, nor is it merciful, to wean on milk such children as must fatten on red meats. Neither is it wise or merciful to wean young soldiers on punishments that would make an Arab woman smile. But still more is it unwise to allow bullies the power of distribution of penalties, for thus comes excess and men punished beyond what they know to be their merits lie back in the harness and so an army falters, then stumbles and finally becomes as nothing.

Still the problem is England's and concerns nobody else, nor is it for others to interfere or criticise. But criticism may be constructive. We may discuss the problem and that leads to conjecture, and to conjecture what would be the public reaction if all the offences punishable by death were known, may be very interesting.

But an active army does not concern itself unduly about public opinion as one can see by the returning gravediggers who pass me by with a clanking of chains as they slowly march manacled to their cells. Returning to the city I purchased for myself a complete set of new garments including uniform and underwear. Though they would only be worn for a week it is good to feel clean again, and decent clothes help one besides being more comfortable. My pay has been accumulating for a long while and I have money awaiting me here from home, so I consider it better to spend this way than waste it all in beer and other useless, though nevertheless pleasurable, ways.

Back at the hotel I filled the bath with hot water and lay back to soak, intending to spend an hour this way. It is a very long time since I have enjoyed such a boon. Growing tired of merely sitting in the water I commenced delousing my old uniform, for it will have to be donned again when I return up the line.

Finally, clean and decently dressed, I sought out Mathews in his room, then wandered out to see what amusement we could suck from this interesting old town.

Cairo to the soldier presents a different aspect from what it does to the tourist. The former can roam and delve in places where the latter never dare go. To the soldier it is a temporary home and he wanders about its streets, absorbs its atmosphere and is as comfortable and at ease as if he were in his home town. Most of us are familiar with all corners of it, know where the best beer is to be had, the best food and where the girls are the prettier. We may not know the names of many streets but it would be next to impossible to lose us in any of them. The glamour and glitter which appeal to tourists has long since worn out for us, but in its stead has grown a familiarity and a liking. One could perhaps better express it as a fascination. We have learned its ways and a smattering of the language; I can find much happiness and pleasurable occupation here as can, I think, all soldiers.

Wandering near the gardens my footsteps automatically turned towards a café hard by where I had spent many happy hours on previous occasions. Finding an outside table we ordered some beer, and sat back at ease; at last our leave is a reality and we intend to enjoy it.

We talk of future intentions, filling each hour so that nothing will be wasted, that we may utilise every moment to the greatest advantage and find the greatest joys and pleasures possible. We have both been here before and know just what we wish to do and where we want to go. Indulging the senses and idly talking can be most entertaining when one has the time and the money too; to look forward and plan when the horizon is clear and no worries present is almost as pleasing as the anticipated indulgences themselves.

As evening draws on we move along in search of food. Our hunger satisfied, we wander about the streets and find ourselves instinctively turning towards the brothel area. It acts as a magnet which always attracts, whether one is actuated by idle time to fill or the need of female society matters not. Whether one's intentions are good or bad it makes no difference, it is part of every soldier's evening amusement and he wanders there if it be only to seek faces he knows. If he does not, the only alternative to wandering the streets is to sit and drink, for Cairo provides little amusement by night other than this for the lowly private.

Though fighting for the preservation of Egypt and the welfare of its inhabitants, we are merely tolerated but neither accepted or appreciated; looked on as a policeman, a sort of necessary nuisance: we are in Egypt but not of it. The civil population wish to have nothing to do with us. The average soldier is a healthy individual with red blood in his veins, and they probably fear for the safety of their daughters, with good reason too in all probability, though this does not greatly concern the soldier, who seems to prefer the brothel, where he is unrestrained. Where if he so desires he may consort with the women or get drunk or anything else his mind dictates. If he forgets he is in civilisation again and acts in a churlish or stupid manner, it affects no one but himself. If he offends the women they are as able to care for themselves as men and retaliate in kind, for they are used to being knocked about.

The civilians are not greatly blamed for their attitude. We are an alien race separated from our kind, doing a tough job which needs tough men, and their resultant actions are but natural with a heterogeneous collection such as we. It comes as a matter of course that the soldier should gravitate to the brothels, where things are freer and easier; more in keeping with his war coarsened mind.

But his constant presence in the brothels should not be misconstrued, for it is by no means always the desire of carnal associations which turns his footsteps towards them. It is often the desire of companionship, to be able to act as one pleases, association with women; for from the beginning of time man has always sought woman, she is necessary to him. Many go there because there is nowhere else to go. Some of us are barely to the age of puberty and are actuated by the insatiable spirit dwelling within us; or craving occupation for the mind, to forget, for a little, war with its misery and sadness.

Much there is in the moral side of war that shocks me, that is an objection to the senses, that shames me to write; but also there is much that remains unwritten that would shock the reader beyond forbearance. That I commit these things to paper and openly discuss them is not with any idea of condoning, or that lewd and bawdy things appeal to me. To the contrary, I find no pleasure in the obscene, it is abhorrent to my sensitiveness. Circumstances compel me, compel us all who dislike to gaze upon them without alternative. I tell of them not as a joy because they hold any pleasure for me, but to build up the case against war. Though the story is woven around a central figure, it is upon the mass that attention should be focused and individuality submerged. He should be regarded as but one, just any one, of the countless hordes that have passed or are passing through the same as I.

Soldiers are attracted by music and dancing, they like to indulge these fancies, and for us this is the only place in Cairo where we can. All the brothels have a reception room where a piano constantly plays to which one can listen, or, if so desiring, dance with the girls. As long as one pays footage by the purchase of beer it is quite unnecessary to consort with the women, for they are only here to make money and they are indifferent whether it is by their bodies or the liquor they sell. Many soldiers move from brothel to brothel, find amusement in each and by the purchase of a few bottles are welcomed every bit as much as he who comes to indulge his cravings.

These light-o'-loves are interesting to study and watch, for many of them have a side to their character which puritan critics would find difficult to believe; but what do they know of such, never having been contaminated by these, to their way of thinking, breeders of bastards and spreaders of disease? Beneath all their veneer they are women and many of them have more womanly instincts than they may be credited with. Many generous actions lie to their credit and the fact of their age-old profession need not necessarily spell utter depravity.

Some once knew good homes, and brought to their present state by white slavery, though many are naturally inclined to the life. But taking them as a whole they may be dissolute and a low crew plying a low trade, who are mostly victims of circumstances. Much depravity exists amongst them and much that is bad and evil, but if one looks with the desire to find, some good is there to be seen.

One sees many peculiar sights, some piteous, others loathsome, many wicked and many that are just ordinary everyday happenings at home, but with the difference that here it is open to be seen whereas at home it is cloaked and hidden One pathetic little tragedy lay at the door of a very well-known girl who had a baby daughter whose father I doubt even she herself knew. She lavished as much love on this kiddie as any decent mother ever did or could. What time she had from her business was spent with it, and of it only she thought and cared.

Usually there is a thrill about the brothel in war time, whether one moves in the white area, or in the black, where the more depraved of the girls dance the can-can. The vitiated air of these places vibrates from the babel of tongues in many languages. Cold thin-blooded people would see only in all this a disgusting debauch but there is something beyond that. It is the scene of the last fling, the anxious groping for joy of miserable desperate men who know they are in all probability going to their deaths in a welter of steel and flame and blood under the hot Syrian skies; perhaps next week or next month, who knows? The war has lasted for years now and, for all they know, may last a dozen more.

The soldiers are so absolutely dependent upon themselves to provide their own amusement and, besides a few mean theatres offering half vaudeville and half pictures, all cheap and not very interesting, there are few places one can go at night, go that one's pleasure evolves into either sitting in the cafés or wandering through the brothels. So it happens that we two find our steps lured in the common direction, and arriving there move from place to place as fancy dictated till eventually we encountered one of the inevitable cafés which Mathews thought he would like to visit.

I was glad of the halt, for pains were commencing to shoot through my stomach. We stayed here awhile, but feeling myself growing worse and not desirous of interfering with Mathews's pleasure I suggested he walk on and I would wait here for him. Getting no better, I called a *gharri,* drove back to our hotel, and dolefully crawled into bed, feeling anything but pleased with such an ending to my first day.

By morning I was completely doubled up, and knowing it was not just a passing belly-ache I crawled out of bed, dressed and set out for the nearest military hospital. One cannot drop in on a chemist here as at home. Finding an orderly, I expected him to give me some physic but unfortunately for my leave he called a doctor, who ordered me off to hospital at once. Not being eligible for admission in Cairo as ours is at Port Said, I must perforce be shipped there.

After a long wait a doctor appears who asks a few questions and goes through the usual tricks they employ for discovering human ailments. To my question as to what the trouble was, he merely shrugs his shoulders and pushes me into a second room. Again I go through the same performance with a second doctor, who instead of answering my very natural question as to what the trouble was, called in an orderly and, pointing to me, said 'Get him a bed.'

The thought of a spell in hospital is not at all undesirable but I would have much preferred that it happened at the end and not the beginning of my leave, for it is almost a certainty that from here I shall go up the line again without any further opportunity of spending the money I have or seeing Cairo again. For many months I have wandered along, surviving on maltreatment and bad and insufficient food. Fever and dysentery have both taken toll of me so that I was near done when leave came. Change of food has brought about the very thing that I had expected, through leave, to avoid: sickness.

Moving away with the orderly I am soon disposed of in a ward with some hundred beds, beds with clean white sheets and real nurses. Seeing Englishwomen again almost makes one forget there is a war, we never see women up the line, but the many broken and sick bodies here dispel the illusion.

My bed is near the doorway along with other dysentery cases so as to be close to the latrines. All day and night an intermittent stream of men is coming and going, some walking, others running.

* * * * * * * *

How good it is to lie here, day after day, with nothing to do! It is hot, but that is nothing unusual. My diet is all soft foods, but as yet I have little interest in what I eat; for days my rations were surreptitiously distributed to men about me and even now I can eat only a little of what is brought me.

The ward is always constant bustle, which provides occupation for the mind more than it annoys. Rest and change of food and altered surroundings too are restoring my perspective. Things are appearing in a different light from a few months back. Happenings which a short while ago would throw me into a rage now scarcely annoy. I can appreciate with better understanding the true value and significance of daily happenings. Gone is that mental twist, that Jordan Valley madness

which so distorts all our ideas. I think of the war and occur-
rences I have been in, but they are less grim now. I often lie for
hours thinking and analysing, fighting past battles and living
amongst almost forgotten joys. Thoughts of war are less bitter,
and those of joys more vivid.

It is perhaps one of the most comforting and consoling dis-
pensations of that power which, for want of a better name, we
call providence, that the mind of man is so constituted as to dwell
on past joys, rather than past pains. True indeed, the sorrows that
are done return at intervals and often with vivid bitterness, but
every recurrence is less cruel than the last and eventually we
can look back at past sufferings with a feeling of humility and
chastened calm which is the beginning of resignation and the
first step to forgetfulness. But the construction of our minds and
memories is such that great happinesses become so interwoven
with the imperishable part of our existence, that they lose   none
of their reality through the passing of time. Anger, hatred and
contentions, suffering and   sorrow, dim and fly away; but the
sunbeams cast by joys of long ago strengthen and become as
strong as the present sun, whilst the very warmth that softened
our harshest moods comes like the evening breeze to settle in
our hearts, softly, gently and tenderly as of yore, and we know
that whilst misery and suffering are the temporary afflictions of
humanity, hope and even pardon and love are an eventual inher-
itance of greater depth and stronger fabric.

So it is that as I lie and think, dream too perhaps, my thoughts
are softened and I think of the common enemy less as a foe and
more as a human being like ourselves. That my mind revolves
amongst things martial is inevitable, for we know of nothing
else, and if I wander through and endeavour to understand past
actions it is more that my mind craves occupation and naturally
runs in the channel it is used to than because it is too steeped in
war to do otherwise.

To think often of the war's end, to seek a bright ray in a
dark sky is comprehensible, it is what we all seek. Recent events
appear in a different light now that I am not actually amongst

them. My brain is clearer and I analyse the campaign and sum up our gains and losses with a mind seeking to understand, toying with a problem the solution of which seems less difficult than the method employed to achieve it leads one to believe.

Men are being removed from this front to bolster up a desperate push in France. We are told they are badly needed there. That too is very true of the position here, so that one cannot help but allow the thoughts to dwell upon this problem, wondering the while if the war will ever end. It seems extraordinary that the Central Powers, comprising but a few nations, can hold the entire world at bay; yet this is the very thing that is happening.

America's recent entry should supply sufficient men to allow us reinforcements, not withdrawals. The fact that Germany and her Allies are withstanding a superior and more diverse army is inconsistent, but nevertheless it is a fact and beneath it lies something that eludes understanding. Whether it be that our High Command is mentally inferior to the German and lacks their strategy, is more than a common soldier such as I can judge; but no matter the reason, there is one. And it seems the more so as the war has dragged itself into 1918, a year it should not have entered.

The prisoners we take are half clothed and fed; it is common to see them with puttee-wrapped feet in lieu of boots; they never seem to have anything new and always seem at a loss to understand why we are so much better cared for. Their first cry when taken is for food. Their ammunition is bad. Quite a number of shells now are duds, equipment too is generally poor, gun barrels are worn; this we know by their erratic shooting even if those we captured did not tell us. That Germany continues the struggle in face of and despite these things is proof of her determination and sincerity. To her this war is the continuance of her very existence; capitulation means finish as an empire.

With us it is different; we are well equipped, and excepting for the extraordinary conditions of the Jordan Valley, are well fed. Our guns are better and fire fewer duds than do the Germans'. Faulty ammunition does occur but this has in some instances been traced to foreign influences at home; once we were issued with paper-filled bullets that fell short of their mark, this more likely is attributable to foreign influence than shortage of materials. Numerically we are the superior force. Treatment in base hospitals could be very much worse; we have behind the line an air of well-being more pronounced than is the case with the enemy. Summing it up we find that the balance lies with us. Yet the war drags on. Why?

We have suffered reverses but with greater numbers of men this might have been averted. Our front is being drained to feed another which has just been strengthened with a new ally; it seems that the pressure is on the wrong spot. Last year's big advance proved that with greater man power it is more than a possibility that we could crush Turkey. It is apparent that if our front was strengthened instead of depleted we would soon be knocking at Germany's back door; Turkey would not be able to withstand us, and with her out of the way we would have a clear passage through. The answer against this may seem to be our poor leadership, or circumstances that we lesser beings are ignorant of.

That our command here is poor is contrary to achieved results. It may be rough in mien and at times unthinking for the men under it, but it nevertheless understands its business and never before has a force been wielded on this front with the skill and determination exhibited now. At times when the tinder refuses to spark it is more than a probability that it has been dampened by the War Office than because the tinder is faulty.

The more one thinks about it the more involved and impossible seems the situation; a couple of nations holding the world at bay and those nations cut off from outside supplies of essential materials whilst we have the world to draw on. Only one angle remains for observation and probably the most likely reason of all, politics. No political party yet was ever entirely unshackled, nor modern British politics. Politicians are invariably governed by those who put them there and whose money keeps them there, so that in some degree we have men who are but puppets, mouthpieces of their masters who are invisible.

The war profiteer desires nothing but the continuance of this strife; human life to him who is far removed from the turmoil is nothing. That a great number of this type of human incubus exists is beyond refute, sufficient of them to wield great influence; for a politician out of power is a man out of work. This resolves the problem in one of personal gain and aggrandisement: which also means continuance of the war, fostered by a steadily growing mandate. If entirely honest military hands were left to guide the helm it is doubtful that the war would still be dragging on, but such is not the case. Instructions come from the Parliament at home as to how best the war can be conducted; these have to be carried out despite apparent irregularity in conception. Should failure arise it is simply said that someone blundered. Usually it is suppressed; but if it becomes public it is not very difficult to find a scapegoat. That the war drags on is not because of lack of supplies, or men, or armaments, or skilful leadership; in all these things we have the advantage. If then these are ruled out but one cause is left and that one is greed.

We rankers are but so many grains of sand, we have nothing to gain and everything to lose. To us the end is eagerly looked for, but daily it grows more elusive. Men are patched up here and sent back to be broken again. A very serious matter for them; but it has a humorous angle in that men are cared for, watched and made new again to be sent out and smashed once more.

Plenty of them are here, in various states of disability. Some get better, others worse. Some will fully recover, others will be cripples, whilst many too will die. Alteration of surroundings make vast differences; in the valley one cared little about life and death, but with returning health and a more sanguine mind, to survive, to get home and forget is the strongest urge I know. The cases about me increase this desire, sights which have become part of a hospital's daily routine serve to bring home how great is the desire to live. Each day we see the operating-theatre-cart take someone away; sometimes they return, but not always. Lying near me till this morning was one with the top clipped off his skull. How he had been brought all this way, had survived the rigours of front line ambulance wagons, and had not succumbed before he covered the hundreds of miles journey, is something that even the doctors do not know. He had become a special case, receiving particular attention because of the medical interest he created. That he could not live with his brain sticking through his head was a certainty. But still he was cared for, though he was never conscious of it, and doctors fought to prolong the life which this morning quietly slipped away. It is really puzzling the sometimes extraordinary contradictions we permit ourselves to accept as normal matters of civilised routine. This man though dying and in pain was kept living, he could not be spared the pain and afforded a merciful death. A man killed in action is nothing, just an everyday occurrence; but if a man is mortally wounded he must be kept alive till he has covered his allotted span.

Another fellow near me had a perforated lung. Though in a bad way his ultimate recovery was expected. A draught caught him which resulted in a fit of coughing till he frothed at the mouth; then he steadily bled. Now he is no more. One man apparently mad was often seen amongst us, we took little notice of his foolish capers. The doctors thought him malingering and did not observe proper care with him. He proved his madness genuine by jumping through a top story window. Yes, there is plenty to occupy one's mind here; something is always happening and death is by no means the least uncommon.

The Red Cross Society are good to us; they supply most of the little necessaries and even luxuries that a soldier needs. They are not niggardly about it either, presenting each man with a list each week of the things they have and giving him what he wants.

When I am able to walk about I move from ward to ward, looking for faces I know and finding many, but nowhere is the one I particularly seek nor does anyone know anything about him. It is most unlikely that he should have gone to any hospital but this, and that I cannot find him here worries me. I have often thought of the way he went and wonder how if perhaps the worst has happened .... I don't know .... I often think of the fellow who jumped through the window.

Watching two orderlies talking this morning, their sudden and spontaneous laughter had surprised me into realising something I have not noticed before. I have listened to many stories and seen many humorous things but always my appreciation was a smile and not a laugh. I cannot remember how long since I have really laughed at anything. The thought is quite startling, I had not believed the valley had gripped me so, had forced even laughter from my soul. To prove myself otherwise I commenced laughing then, to the consternation of nearby patients who wondered what ailed me. Now I think of it, I cannot remember any of us finding laughter in anything since that cursed valley enwrapped us.

* * * * * * * *

On the water's edge of Port Said is our rest camp; from the hospital we come here to gain strength before moving out to the details and so up the line. Each day we swim; in fact, I do nothing else but lie in the sun or swim in the sparkling water. We do not worry about costumes for we are detached from beaten paths and no one troubles us here. One morning I swim too far along the beach and some civilians come down before I can return and I have no alternative but to swim through them.

Next day I buy a costume so that I may swim the full length of the beach and mix with the bathers farther along. At first they take no notice of me, then suddenly I find I am alone; wherever I move they go away. I cannot understand it and wonder what there is about me that frightens them. I observe myself and can find nothing to alarm them till I see my identity disc hanging about my neck. This little tag tells everyone that I am a soldier and as such to be avoided. It is not desirable that I should mix with them: it is always the same, they fear for their women.

If one is walking down the street and a lone woman approaches she will pass to the other side, for she fears she may be accosted if the street is deserted; life is not easy for women here, the law regarding the looser type is so strict. They are allowed to ply their trade only within the prescribed area; to do so elsewhere invites a severe penalty. A woman spoken to in the street may evoke suspicion and she may be called on to explain. If it were found she consorted with men and aroused the suspicion that she was a prostitute, she would be immediately classed as one and segregated to the defined area. It is also liable to give their friends doubts of their professed decency.

We have huts run by various organisations wherein one can read and find occupation of a quiet nature; they are scattered in different parts of the town. Passing one of these at night I was induced by the strains of a familiar tune to venture inside, the music suggesting fellowship and possibly somebody I knew. It was a Sunday night and the music of a semi-sacred nature accompanied by masculine voices of soldiers from the camp nearby. Standing within the door glancing around for faces I knew, I suddenly, as the music stopped, found myself the centre of attention. The pianist had recognised me and, disregarding the task in hand, had abruptly ceased playing, scrambled from the platform and with wild impetuosity thrust a passage through the bewildered singers till he reached where I stood, to embrace me, as one long lost. It was a fellow who had been in camp with me back home; we had been good friends and spent most of our time together, but had been drafted to different units and drifted apart. It was like a breath of home to see this old familiar face and opened up an immediate avenue of friendly talk forgetful of the audience, or should it be termed congregation? Arm in arm we passed through the door and down to the centre of the town, sought out a secluded table and over our beer exchanged such news as the vicissitudes of war made interesting.

That I should have unearthed my friend playing the piano for a Sunday evening hymn service was not at all surprising. He had a kink that way. Back home in our country camp he was a very staunch member of the local Salvation Army, being their accepted organ player. He could never resist music in any form and dearly loved to be the musician. One night he had offered to play the *Army* organ which offer was accepted, and from then onwards such nights as he had leave would always find him at this. Back at their citadel he performed the same function and had even gone to the length of permitting himself to be saved, he who had not one religious bone in his body, but in doing so he became their accepted organist. It was his boast that he had been saved more than any other man, which was probably nearly true. It was this passion for music that had lured him into playing where I had just met him, but his desire to play could wait and the demand on him as pianist for the hymn service was of second importance when an old friend and some beer were waiting to be enjoyed. His hymn playing, simply that he might indulge his passion for music, in no way affected his religious feelings; it is very doubtful if he had any and he played with utter disregard of the sacred character of the occasion. Had anything upset him whilst doing so he would burst into a torrent of language, as I had once seen him do, then apologise profusely to the padre in charge, not because he was sorry but to alleviate the wounded feelings of that worthy. This peculiar mania of his reminded me sadly of Smith with his Bible-leaf cigarette papers, which he smoked with perfect equanimity and with no regard for their sacred nature.

Down a quiet street in a backwash, little frequented by the cosmopolitan crowd that is Port Said, hides a café rejoicing in the name of *La Fleur de Nuit* though what sort of flower one can wonder. Towards it my friend Jones led me. He spoke highly of its entertainment, and knowing Jones as I do, that suggested that I might expect anything.

Entering the narrow door unencumbered by the usual cluster of tables so beloved by the French, we descended some half-dozen steps into a large room low ceilinged and brightly lit by unshaded lights from overhead cross beams. Tables and chairs were scattered around the floor against the walls, leaving a clear space for those who desired dancing to the mutilated music ground out by an old man and two young-old girls on a harp, 'cello and violin, though one would have difficulty in recognising the instruments by their sound.

A number of soldiers were careering around performing what they believed was a waltz, dancing with each other as girls were scarce. Seeking a table, Jones was spun amongst a group of sitters by an exuberant couple of Scots, not at all sure of their feet, as legs made shaky by bad wine led them an erratic course across the floor.

Picking himself up he turned aggressively to the Scots, to be met with an embrace and a request to have a dance. Preferring a seat, which seemed the safer course, we all four accommodated ourselves in a corner and accepted an invitation to drink bad wine. Shortly we were joined by two English Transport men, so forming quite an imperial group, all determined to make it a big night, immediately friendly though we had never met till a moment agone; but such is camaraderie.

One Scot, tired of a male dancing-partner, insisted that the violinist join him. She, used to such things, laughed and continued her lament accompanied by the Scot's earnest requests in his own Arabic-French to come and dance with him, whilst she reiterated that she did not speak Scotch but thoroughly understood English. The proprietor, unable to reason with him, appealed to the company to persuade the gentleman not to interfere with the music. We insisted that the girl comply, which was acceded to as the only way to restore order.

The pair whirled amongst the chairs till exhaustion finally stayed their efforts. The Scot then insisted that his partner sing; and this too was granted for the sake of order. It was a popular song in French with a swinging lilt, its name unknown to me.

Not to be outdone, at its conclusion our friend stepped on to a table and broke into *Annie Laurie*. Seeming so absorbed in its theme he perceptibly sobered as he sang, whilst we listened in silence as he poured out with pathos this glorious air of the heather. At its conclusion silence reigned for minutes, hardened men overcome, their minds miles away from present dingy surroundings. A thunder of applause and our friend rejoined us, toasts were drunk and the business of the night proceeded.

A little Cockney at a table nearby bawled a comedy song, ground it out with effort and no sign of ending till someone quietened him by throwing the contents of a glass into his open mouth—what waste!

As the night wore on the din increased till a patrol of military police appeared just as our two Transport friends were staging a friendly wrestle for the company's entertainment. They were seized and marched away for having caused a disturbance.

We remaining four held a hurried conference and decided on immediate rescue. Building our party up to seven, we snatched some chairs as we passed out into the streets. Breaking them into handy weapons we rushed by devious ways to come ahead of the patrol and catch them unawares.

From the shadows where we hid we fell on them as they passed, rescued our newly-made friends, and departed our several ways to camp.

* * * * * * * *

A week by the water; and one day a train takes me back to our details where, after only one day, I join a batch going up the line. The spell in hospital was very good and I am duly grateful for it, but nevertheless regret my lost leave and the high lights missed in Cairo.

We travel to Kantara in the luxury of a third-class coach; officers always travel first, non-coms second, and we nobodies third. When in small batches we have the temerity to go second, which flagrant infringement of military law brings much trouble on our heads. The native inspectors are always accompanied by military police who take great pleasure in ejecting us, that is if we are not in too great force. If this be the case they wait till the first station where assistance can be obtained. Through this insistence that we travel third numerous scuffles occur, sometimes resulting in the police being thrown from the moving train, but unfortunately they are seldom hurt because of the soft sand.

Excepting soldiers, only the very low caste natives travel third, and because of them we object. They are always stinking and filthily lice-ridden, as too are the carriages from contact with them. The authorities insist that a clear distinction must be drawn between ranks, which is the why and wherefore of it all; it is ever so. In the eyes of brass-hats we are only so much dirt.

At Kantara we cross on foot the pontoon bridge spanning

the canal and march towards the troop train awaiting us. The carriages now are all open trucks with but wooden awnings overhead to break the severity of the sun's rays. The only distinction is that officers have their own truck separate from the rabble, and if they be of sufficiently high rank they have a real passenger coach.

Marching along we pass detachments of prisoners mending roads; fat and well fed, their faces reflecting with moon-like contentment the satisfaction they derive from this peaceful incarceration, it is no hardship to them. The work is nominal and they live in perfect safety with regular food. It is almost unnecessary to guard them; they are not likely to desert or run away; their lives are better here than ever, either as peasants before or soldiers during the war.

The only thing they lack is female association. It is hard on any nationality to be closed away like this from feminine contact, human instincts are the same the world over; women are as necessary to the Turks as to the Briton or to any man. These men have been used to their indulgences; the fact of being a prisoner does not alleviate that want; to the contrary, the climate here increases it. Doubtless, though, they have their means of satisfaction.

It is an amazing place this Kantara; before the war only a name and a few hovels, now a mass of depôts, prison camps, dumps and all the paraphernalia necessary to an army. The troops quartered here come from all corners of the globe, ranging from the pale yellowy brown of the Egyptian and the white skin of Britons to the ebony black of Abyssinians. Italy and France are represented not only by their own sons but also by the peoples of their colonies scattered throughout Africa. From the British Empire come we Colonials, Hindoos, Sudanese and many others. A more motley collection of colours, or a more diverse intermingling of languages and creeds would be difficult to find, whilst scattered everywhere are the British Tommies. Running through all this gathering of dumps and depôts, like strands in a tangled skein, are miles upon miles of railways and countless shunting lines and sidings, covering many many acres. It would be very easy to become lost in the maze and not be able to ask one's way from more than one in every five because of the hopelessly mixed nationalities camped here.

Finding our train, a frenzied rush commences to secure the best positions, not seats, for the trucks are devoid of anything of that nature. We are far in excess of the accommodation provided (which is usually the case) and we pack in like so many sardines in a tin. It is not possible for everyone to sit; many take up half-standing half-squatting postures, crammed in as best we can with our equipment slung to the roof, to the buffers, or else hung over the side. Very soon the train gathers way and we draw out into the open and lonely desert, once more bound for the vast beyond that lies out here from Kantara.

It is unlikely that we will be less than two days travelling, and being so cramped we soon turn to means of increasing our comfort or, to be more exact, to decrease our discomfort. Bivouac sheets are opened and erected on top of the wooden awnings overhead, a rifle each end for support and the little tent is complete. The congestion relieved, we seek occupation, mostly in talk or cards.

Stopping at a wayside station, the R.T.O. objects to our tents and refuses permission for the through passage of the train till they are removed and those of us on top climb within the trucks. A useless and senselessly unnecessary order, for it is apparent to all how cramped we are; besides which this is the accepted form of travel in desert trains. If he will not permit the train to start, we don't particularly care, for it is of little consequence to us if we never reach our destination. He calls upon two officers travelling with us who have been watching the proceedings with detached unconcern; they merely smile and tell him it is his affair; he began it. His dignity upset, he retires to his bell-tent office. The train waits and no signal to move; the engineer blows his whistle and gives a few convulsive shunts but still the railway flunky sulks. Finally the engine-driver, grown tired of the nonsense, gradually opens his throttle and we roll on through the desert, over country that has been a battlefield, every mile of it wrested from the Turk. In those days we had no railway, it has been laid behind us like a long thread as we advanced.

As we have all come from Egypt, talk as we settle down is mostly of our doings there. Beer and rum appear in a surprising manner and, our tongues gradually loosened, we talk of the good times we have had; often voices are raised in argument over the relative merits or demerits of this and that, generally some woman of the brothels, many of whom are better known than the Rock of Gibraltar. Even the most puritan know these different girls, for no matter how virtuous a soldier may be, no man that ever wore a uniform here has not been amongst them, though not necessarily associated with them.

Discussion evolves about many things, anecdotes are told, reminiscences unfolded. In our truck are men from three countries, all British. They have seen the relics of ancient days, the Sphinx, the Pyramids, but who wishes to talk of that. They are but average men with normal vices. To consort with women, drink and generally play the game to the utmost limit is all the joy that comes into their lives; they are open about it and make no secret of these things. Most of these men have done at home what they discuss having done here; as coming generations will continue to do. The difference between the soldier and the civilian is to be measured in hypocrisy. The former has passed the stage of caring and his vices are apparent for all to see, whereas the latter does these things in secret and therefore is less man than hypocrite.

Conversation may be crude but is essentially true for all that and it is but representative of the average soldier. It reflects his pleasures, his vices; his reactions under given conditions; little is applicable to the few. It is to be remembered that men constantly playing with fate, never knowing what each day will bring, seeing death in their daily routine and with the courage to laugh at it, could not be in a normal state of mind.

The high tension under which a soldier lives requires an outlet and when he finds an escape for his feelings, the natural impulse is to make all he can of it, for he never knows what lies ahead. He lives for the day only, often doubting if he will see tomorrow and when he does, wondering how. A great army of men is constituted of varied temperaments; out of this hurly burly the average arises and by it they are judged, not the extremes. Many keep themselves uncontaminated, others go to the opposite length. Neither of these two classes are indicative of an army, though the former are to be praised as much as the latter are to be eschewed; it is the man in the middle that counts.

He is one of a mass and acts with them; he swims with the tide, neither good nor bad, just a homeless exile playing with fate. Leave to him means a few days respite during which he endeavours to keep the past from his mind; to have a good time, to create something to think of when it is over. He is not able to go home and see his kin; his leave is spent amongst strangers, which leaves it incumbent on himself to find his own pleasures, so he does as others do.

Soldiers are like people with uneasy consciences inasmuch as they desire to forget; so they take life as it comes and make the most of it. Play the hazard always, in battle or in pleasure. To understand the motives behind a soldier's many actions requires a mind attuned to his. Unless you have been amongst it, felt that clammy hand upon your heart, heard the shrieks and known the agonies of it all, how can you judge, you who have not seen?

War is a gruesome business true enough, but it has its lighter moments, as indeed has every serious undertaking. When under the actual strain of fire we think of nothing but the agony of it all, yet when released from that strain and the fear of it removed we find much good in life and think the old world not such a bad place after all. That our minds are seared by its ghastliness is beyond doubt, and this probably accounts for the whole-hearted abandon with which a soldier takes his pleasures, even to excessiveness.

I think I have long ago become a fatalist, and think it better one should believe that things are ordained and do not happen by chance; for then one can face the future and withstand the

154

horrors of warfare with greater calm that he who expects every moment to bring the end. Believing in the fixed order of events eventually gives a man that greater mental stolidity of knowing that his span is allotted and will not end till its appointed time, no matter to what risks he is exposed, so that because of this we, who think that way, can face death with greater temerity, knowing that if it is not our time we cannot be harmed – but that if our span be ended we must bow down to it; for nothing that we may do can alter matters ordained.

The longer I live and the more I see of the coarser side of war, the less becomes my revulsion. It is not so long since, that much filled me with abhorrence and nausea and many happenings called up in me a feeling of rebellion that things should be so. Constant contact and an ever-increasing philosophic fatalism has given me the strength to take as a matter of course these things that once were so repugnant. I have lost the desire to rail against war's gruesomeness, or to object to its seemingly unnecessary restrictions, and in becoming this way my mind is possessed of a greater calm and an increased ability to face everything. A philosophic acceptance of unavoidable happenings is a solace which those who possess it are the better for. It may be that long contact has inured me against the things which once so upset me, but I think that is only part of the reason. I have learned to treat a mangled corpse, a pariah-chewed body, carnage and devastation with greater equanimity than when first I moved amongst such things; they no longer raise in me rebellion, and I am the better for it.

It is a change that has been gradual, so much so that I had not noticed the metamorphosis, it is only that sights once causing revulsion now are accepted; and the discovery of this fact brings me face to face with this change, so gradual that I realised not the transition, only the accomplished fact now that it has occurred.

I had been sitting in a corner turning these things over in my mind, half oblivious of my surroundings till a voice penetrated to my inner consciousness asking someone if he remembered the place we were passing. Hearing no immediate answer,

I looked across to the questioned who was staring out over the shimmering desert. Turning his head he asks 'Why?' 'Don't you remember the Tommy we found spread-eagled when out here in a patrol?,' the first queries.

'Oh, yes, I remember that, and when we rode up and began to cut him down, he asked to be left, saying his punishment would only be increased if we interfered!'

'We cut him down though,' the first speaker interrupted, 'and a Tommy officer came up and threatened to report us, and we told him that we had a good mind to put him up as a substitute for the Tommy. I wonder what happened to the poor devil, we never came back that way again.'

'Whoever introduced that bloody torture should be crucified himself, but with real nails' broke in a burly artilleryman of the H.A.C.

It is a fact, and an abhorrent one too, but none the less true for that, that this barbarous practice should survive as a means to inflict inhuman torture on un-defensive soldiery. Invented two thousand years ago, used for the crucifixion of Christ, condemned through history's pages as an everlasting blot on Jewry, yet perpetrated now in a modified form by those who condemn.

Often the crime was not of great proportions. The guilty man would be tied to a limber wheel so as to form the letter X with his limbs and left to the mercy of the boiling sun. A little while and the strength is sapped; the prisoner droops, then hangs by his hands, his feet no longer able to support him. What pain it inflicts only those who have seen it practised know. I remember a battalion of infantry who had been in India since the outbreak of war and were staying in Egypt for a few weeks waiting transport to France. They were permanent soldiers and had collected a goodly number of souvenirs from the former country. Transport being so scarce, baggage had been cut to a minimum so that a good deal of their gear must be dumped. The officers, having many skins and heads, garnered during their long sojourn in India and being reluctant to part with them, cut down the baggage allowance of the rank and file to their bare equipment, by which means a surplus of space was created so that commissioned ranks were able to retain their trophies. An act of selfishness parallel with many English units who carried collapsible bath tubs, beds and other unnecessary impedimenta for officers' convenience, at the expense of the common herd. In the desert haulage is exceedingly difficult and to fill the waggon trains with such junk meant that no space was available for privates, who must needs carry their all on their backs and in consequence do with less.

******** *

As night comes and darkness sinks on the unfriendly desert we squirm into as comfortable positions as we can and try to sleep. The train shunts and stops many times, and seems bent on doing all it can to keep us awake. Morning bursts with glad relief to all, for sleep in a troop train is more an expression than a possible accomplishment.

As day wears on the country undergoes a gradual change as we pass from the desert to the firmer soil of Southern Palestine. Later signs of scattered habitations appear, then cultivated patches, and as we go still farther North, sown fields and villages, near one of which the train stops. Some of the more venturesome clamber from the trucks and stretch their legs, not along the line but away towards the village. Whilst we watch them, having nothing else to occupy our attention, we notice them lifting large globular things from a cultivated patch. It does not take us remaining in the train long to recognise them as water melons, something that I at least have not seen for ages. Very soon the train is emptied, as a hurried scramble commences to obtain some of these more than welcome melons; even the train crew come along.

As we wander back to the train, occupied only in eating the fruit (the Jewish inhabitants screeching at us meanwhile), a military police patrol unexpectedly arrives. *Ubique* would be a fitting motto for these gentry, they crop up in the most unthought-of places. Not more than six of them, they remonstrate and threaten but of no avail. In return we revile and pelt the skins at them, some even going to the length of walking towards them so that, as they are chased back, the police come within the range of those in the trucks. The engine driver, thinking we have had enough, blows his whistle and we steam away leaving the unhappy police threatening to wire ahead about us. This perturbs us not at all, as with men so scarce it is most unlikely the authorities would consider gaoling a train load.

From this village the journey remained fairly monotonous till we arrived at the base of the hills leading up to Jerusalem, where Mathews and I had been fed by the canteen sergeant. Not unmindful of my mental promise to that good fellow I had brought a bottle of rum for him. Being told the train would wait an hour I went in search of my good Samaritan and duly finding him presented my bottle, much to his gratification. In the meantime our trains had been changed so that the troops would not be kept waiting longer than necessary. This resulted in my being left behind, which I discovered to my consternation on returning to the siding. In peace times we miss hundreds of trains and it matters little, but here it is an entirely different matter; if I am discovered absent at Jerusalem it means criming and a penalty. Returning to my canteen sergeant I explained the situation to him. He treated it as a good joke, but nevertheless spared no trouble to overcome my predicament. Finding the guard of the next train up which shortly was leaving, he committed me to his care and soon I was once again on my journey. The guard was a capital fellow, a Tommy belonging to the Railway Corps. As he was permanently stationed at the one place he had been able to make friends with nearby Jews and so enjoyed a greater degree of comfort than others less fortunate. To what extent this comfort lent itself was duly evident when he suggested we should eat. From a hamper he produced a chicken, some fruit, bread and two bottles of wine, all of which was consumed to the last crumb, a veritable feast for me.

After our meal he left me to patrol along the trucks. Being a food train, robbery by natives on the slow-going up-grades was a very common occurrence, and this patrol was accordingly carried out with a loaded rifle. On this trip no marauders were discovered, but shortly after his return the draw-bar connecting his brake van snapped, leaving us to career madly backwards down the hill. The guard soon applied the brake, but we had no means of acquainting the engine crew of our dilemma and in consequence had to wait nearly an hour till they discovered our absence and came shunting back searching for us.

No other excitement occurred to liven the journey and so about midnight we steamed into Jerusalem. Bidding my new-found friend good-bye, I went in search of the details camp, hopeful to sneak in before my absence was discovered. Next morning we were transported in lorries down to Jericho where horses waited to take us up the valley to our various units.

CHAPTER 11

RIDE OUT TO CONQUER

Even after Egypt's heat, this place greets one with a hot caress like the breath from a furnace. Leaving Jericho after midday, it is almost dark when finally I come to my troop lines, and am allotted to a section; of my old one there seems to be no sign. Seeking for familiar faces, I peer first into one bivouac then another, many of the faces I know but they are mostly of comparatively new men. The regiment is back a little from the front line and men move about with less care than otherwise would be the case; lights are visible in the bivouacs, though shielded nevertheless. The troop has changed even in the few short weeks I have been away, I can see; it is not the old troop, not the troop that originally came down to the valley; it never will be that again. No one looks forward to this death-ridden valley; the only joy we have in returning is the friendships of our comrades. I feel alone, destitute, the friends I had expected I cannot find. Moving from shelter to shelter I see many faces that I know, but not the old hands I seek. Peering into one I espy Lenny; it is good to see his ugly dial again. So good that I almost embrace him and quickly ask after first this one and then that one. He speaks of all whom I mention; some are still here but with others it is all the same, the fever. His face looks like a skull with parchment stretched over it. Leaving him a minute I move outside and rummage amongst my gear, returning with a bottle of rum. Reading the label his face lights up, his obvious pleasure and almost childish joy will make it taste the sweeter. Rum in the valley is worth its weight in gold; more than that, for we have money but no rum.

Two others creep into the bivouac, fellows I am glad to see. I produce my second and last bottle. We drink and talk far into the night; better to drink now for tomorrow—who knows?

Friendship is one of the greatest things in our lives, one thing that fever, wounds or hardships cannot break, only death and even then the memory lingers on. We are all joined together by a common cause living in toleration for each other; small coteries spring up, little groups form, attracted together by compatibility. Mateships are formed which mean very much to us. Many of these mateships on the surface seem incongruous, it is not always apparent what they have in common, especially when composed of men who are opposites in natures, upbringing and thought, yet a tie runs underneath which is more binding than blood. Very often men of equal or similar civil status are attracted to each other which is natural, their minds are attuned alike; but it is not always so. We have a couple here who mentally are poles apart yet two brothers were never dearer to each other, were never less selfish to one another or more tolerant. One is a clergyman turned lawyer, a god-fearing man, morally and mentally clean, whilst his companion is a dyed-in-the-wool rogue, a rascal of the hooligan type. They never offend each other's susceptibilities or ever criticise, though the roughness of one is often an irritation to his friend. That he strives to moderate it and pattern himself upon his less boisterous mate is token of his regard and that this reformation is observed but never commented on, proof of his friend's goodwill and fellowship and desire to help.

We have many in the ranks who are men of consequence at home, more than one is a landowner and many are sons of wealthy graziers. We have one here whose boon companion was a coal miner. College men in the ranks are common, our troop owns to two university undergraduates.

These friendships, peculiar as many of them seem but none the less sincere for that, are such that can withstand every vicissitude of our disordered lives, are proof against petty jealousies or any occurrence that otherwise may disrupt them if it were not for their very strength. They ride on, supremely above quarrels which only tend to cement them the more, and are deaf to all intrigue that would affect them. One's quarrels are his friend's quarrels, irrespective of their right or wrong; loyalty demands that.

Our souls, our minds, our hearts are laid bare in this arena of war, our good and our bad have at some time been displayed for all to see, we have no illusions about each other, we know one another's value to the last degree. In forming our friendships we know exactly the calibre of those we mix with, there never can be an undetected something to crop up later and wreck our illusions. Our friendships have been tested by many twists and contortions in war's melting pot, heated and reheated in its crucible, kneaded and cemented under conditions never normal so that once mutually bound there is nothing that can rend asunder. Life knows nothing more beautiful, more holy to those who contract it, more binding than the most solemn oath. It is the greatest thing that has come, or is coming out of this war. It rises to unreachable pinnacles, far above the sordidness of our common earthly existence, the very heat in which its seed germinated has purified it from contamination. It stands for all that is good in us, knows no meanness or selfishness, is emblematical of our steadfast regard for those whom we know as mates and will live on till death, and we are the better for it.

* * * * * * * *

I think I must have grown soft whilst away from here, but two days back and I feel the old burning in my veins again. Each day it grows more troublesome, fits of giddiness compelling me to stop what I am doing and cling to a support whilst everything goes around in a circle.

We have a wicker hut now for those with the fever, one is placed there till it either becomes too bad and he is removed, or else it subsides sufficiently to permit one's return to the line. It is run on lines similar to a hospital with room for twenty men; it is always full, with men lying under canvas shelters outside. The interior is bare, except for a table on which the food is mixed and the quinine bottle stands; we receive endless quantities of that. No beds are provided, patients lying huddled together on the earth floor, which is covered only by each patient's blanket. Each morning men come and go here, everybody in his turn; it is unavoidable here in the valley; a few days, then back to the line again, or else out to hospital; no one stays long. Sanitation is our usual method, a long pit nearby. Conditions allow only the scantiest attention; it is more a place of observation than a hospital. We do not grumble at its scant comfort, but are thankful to have somewhere to lie and somebody to feed us.

A few days of rest in this shelter and I am once more in my accustomed place, fulfilling the usual fatigues, laying endless miles of barbed wire, and performing the usual patrols and reconnaissances.

A line of wire runs across our front from the foothills to the river. In its middle a break has been purposely created, known as the gap. Every night outposts watch this wire, with a listening-post out in advance of the gap; the intention being that should the enemy attack he will feel along the wire till he finds the break, coming through there he will make contact with the listening post who will give the alarm by rifle fire. The gap is the trap, and the listening post the bait which, in the event of night-attack, meets the usual fate of baits.

Behind the wire-work are a number of consolidated positions, empty by day but fully manned at night. The scrubby bushes growing in profusion at this end of the valley have necessitated a maze of wire-work; they provide excellent cover for a creeping enemy.

These constant nightly outposts, with the resultant nerve strain, weary us more than actual labour. We are beginning to dread them, particularly the listening post, the certainty of annihilation on that particular duty should the enemy attack greatly enhances the hazard and naturally our antipathy to this job; fortunately it is long in repeating itself once we have performed it.

When last I was a member of the party detailed for this unenviable task we met with a little distraction which on previous occasions other men had also encountered. Riding out at darkness we dismounted at the wire and completed the journey on foot, leaving the horses, whose jangling bits and stamping feet were always liable to attract unwanted attention. Moving from bush to bush like so many shadows, we hugged what cover we could find till near the post, when we crept forward on our bellies, being very near the Turkish line.

Two men watch together here because of the nerve strain. We had hardly ensconced ourselves when distinctly to our ears came the sound of rustling bushes. What it portended we soon discovered as a Turkish post came into view, they saw us very soon after we observed them. Each party kept the other covered, the Turks in the meantime taking up a position not far from us. Neither party dare fire while night lasted, we for fear of rousing the entire line, as out here our only means of communication and attracting attention was by fire and would immediately precipitate an action, the Turks too in all probability actuated by the same fears. It is uncanny to see the enemy so close, not fifty paces away, watching us as intently as we watch them, faces clearly distinct in the moonlight and though opposed neither party daring to fire; we are the eyes and ears of all behind us. A disconcerting sound attracts our attention; it is believed wild pigs sometimes frequent the river bed; I do not know if it is so, but it would account for strange noises we hear there sometimes at night. In our imagination small noises are magnified, it is a nerve-racking business and the waning night seems long in dragging to its weary end. At the first suggestion of the day, the Turks commenced falling back; but we remained watchfully still, covering their movements. The lead horses coming up meantime, we mount and chase after the Turks now dangerously near their line. As we gallop up one turns and fires, but quickly we are on them and they all elevate their hands except the one who fired; our officer commanding had ridden him down before he fired again.

We feel a little vengeful towards them because they fire and surrender in almost one action. As we near our wire a Turkish patrol appears in the rear, and a troop of ours is quickly after them; it is common to follow our posts in as we had done the Turkish. We pass a dead Turk, probably sniped the previous day, he had not begun to swell, nor did he stink. We have not time to bury him so we drag him along with us.

Lenny is walking about with his feet swathed in Turkish puttees; he has the foot-rot through excessive sweat which runs down the legs into his boots, and rots the flesh from under the toes. It is very painful, making the toes like hot coals; I have it a little too—who hasn't? The flesh seems to perish, and can be scraped from under the toes with the finger nails till the bones are almost laid bare. It is very unwise to do this, but it is very satisfying.

The quartermaster must have opened his heart today; we have received a double tobacco issue. Not many cigarettes, mostly rolling tobacco; we buy papers and make our own. It is most essential to have the wherewithal to smoke; we can do without many things but not that.

Some mail has come too. We eagerly cluster around as the names are read out. I do not notice if some names are not called and men disappointed. I am too intently listening for my own. Letters are not always agreeable, they often bring bad news from home. We are so far away that small matters are apt to become exaggerated in our minds. I look for papers, something to read; when one is free a paper is good to have; we tire of talking, we have used up all matters of interest long ago, and our diversions are very limited. Newspapers are passed around, every line of them is read, even the advertisements too.

When the last name is called we go to our bivouacs and read what the letters say. This does not take long but it provides conversation for many hours; we tell each other what they are about. In one letter of mine is a casualty list in which our regiment figures. I read down the names I know and a lump comes in my throat. I search for one name but it is not there, then I pass it on for others to see. Another tells of a parcel sent me by a previous mail; I have not received it, perhaps it has become lost in the post; they sometimes disappear that way, or at the base.

Two planes circle overhead, the sun scintillating on their wings. Lazily they move as if the heat even at that altitude is too much for them. One draws away and flies from sight, the other continues its languid circling; the roar of the exhaust increasing and dying as it comes and goes.

I lie sheltered from the sun's rays but every now and then the plane comes across my vision. At first I watch it as one might a fly crawling along a ceiling, but the effort of that soon wearies me. The flies buzz around with annoying persistence; a piece of bush with which I constantly swish does not seem to perturb them.

The plane roars back again; as it does so its exhaust grows louder, then alternates in volume with the quickness of its evolutions. I strain my neck to see why it is manoeuvring and find two of them, but on one is the black cross of Germany. I watch them fascinated as they twist and struggle for position, the rattle of their machine-guns distinctly audible.

One minute they are high up, the next swooping low to the ground, each striving to come above the other. The German pulls away turning to his own lines with ours in pursuit. Little white puffs surround them as the anti-aircraft shells burst, but they continue out of sight, apparently contemptuous of the futile efforts of the ground guns.

The diversion they have provided over, I creep back into my shelter. Scrapping planes always provide a thrill to us onlookers; we watch and hope to see the enemy plane crash from on high with seldom a thought for the pilots falling to their deaths, the primitive in us aroused by this most thrilling of all combats.

Our air force had once been inferior to the enemy's, but has since been improved and has grown till now we hold the upper hand. Daily they patrol from the valley to the coast so that no enemy observation behind our lines is possible. Rumours of a gigantic advance soon to be attempted are lent colour to by this never relaxing vigilance.

* * * * * * * *

We are to vacate this sector and exchange with units along the river bed down near the bridgehead. It is possible that the severe strain of the heat has necessitated this; we could not last much longer, another month and there would be no one left.

Riding along the semblance of a track to Jericho we pass a battalion of Tommy infantry coming up the valley. Marching with their heads hanging, faces and clothes begrimed and thick with dirt, they pass in a cloud of blinding choking dust. No cheery nod or salutation as they go by, they have long since exceeded all limits of caring. We watch them with feelings of pity, we know what they suffer in this sweltering heat. The sweat oozes out of them mixing with the dust to form a coating of mud on their clothes and faces. They are new to the valley and only know it by repute till now. We are hardened through months of it and sympathise with them on their introduction to the devil's playground. They pass in a daze, only their grit keeping them going; there are no bands and cheering crowds to watch them. We move aside and halt to avoid adding more dust to their torment then return to the road as the last of the column disappears.

As we do so we find some who have dropped in their tracks and have been left behind, unconscious, on the road. Why they are deserted we do not know, it is a barbarous thing to do and we are very annoyed about it. It shows mighty little consideration from their leaders that no provision has been made for cripples and they are left to the sun's mercy like this; a few hours of it and they would be finished completely.

Our commanding officer grows heated about it and is very terse in his comments; he will have something to say to Headquarters when he reaches Jericho. A detail is left behind to care for them till they recover and are able to be brought back for treatment. We are not surprised at the colonel's wrath; anything savouring of callousness from officer to man always raises his ire. He regards a ranker as a human being, not as a mere automaton and treats him accordingly. He has never been above conversation with his men, which has made him popular and commands our greater respect.

At the bridgehead the campaign enters a new phase. The ordinary front line routine is carried out as usual but in addition we make the first moves in a huge game of bluff. Each night details spread out over the valley floor to light innumerable little fires to give the impression of incoming troops. Countless tents are erected and horse lines laid down to which are tethered make-believe horses. By day men move about these dummy camps to give an air of occupancy. A few live horses, mostly old crocks, are placed on the lines to provide movement and give life to the delusion. The fake ones are simply four uprights erected at an angle with a cross piece over which a blanket is draped. Behind all this lies a reason, a very deep reason. It is a delusion especially provided to mislead the Turks and Germans into believing another attack is premeditated from the valley, our two previous attempts to scale the plateau lending weight to this.

As we people the valley with imaginary soldiers, the coastal sectors are being filled with real men. By day the roads are quiet, at night they come to life, and till morning witness scenes of feverish activity. A great movement of troops to the coast goes forward coming from all parts of the line, whilst the valley, instead of being strengthened as the Turk believes, is in reality being depleted.

We have sledge-like arrangements which we tie behind horses and drag about in the dust, raising it in great clouds till it so completely envelopes us that the Turk cannot see it is but a few men, for this we are often shelled but that is part of our everyday existence. Everything that brains can devise is called into operation to add to this colossal bluff.

We curse and sweat ourselves even thinner than we thought it possible to be as we go about this killing work; it is no joke to us who drag the sledges in the heat. We have an inkling of what is to come, but our brains have been grilled here too long to find much amusement in the anticipated discomfiture of the Turk when the mask is drawn. The one consolation it does give us is the possibility of complete victory, when the advance goes forward and the opportunity of repayment; we have a score of still unsettled-for past reverses up on those heights. . . .

After a gruelling day drawing dust ploughs our troop pull into a dummy camp to light the usual fires. It has been very hot and we are thirsty. Walking towards a *wadi* bed nearby for water, I am hindered by some bushes through which I crawl to the water's edge. As I kneel down in the darkness my hand slips, precipitating me into the stream. Clambering out I fill my bottles then take a long draught of the evil-tasting water before returning to the lines.

Next morning I discover the reason of a peculiar smell I had noticed when filling the bottles, also why the water was tainted. On its side in the *wadi* bed lay the remains of a camel. Its flesh had either putrefied away, or else had been eaten by the creatures that live and thrive on such carrion. I had filled my bottles and drunk from where its belly had once been.

Returning to the bridgehead we hear shells whistling overhead from the great naval gun the Turks use daily to shell Jericho. These *coal buckets* are of no consequence to us, for the target is never varied.

Near the river our dust brings down the fire from a number of field pieces; we canter our horses forward and soon are out of range amongst the network of mounds along the Jordan's bed.

Passing in front of a cluster of stunted trees one of our own sixty-pounder batteries opens fire as we pass right under the barrels. So well had they been camouflaged we had not observed their presence and were temporarily deafened by the concussion. Blackboy, except for a shake of the head and a quiver, shows no perturbation. Coming up to our horse lines, the shelling recommences so that we quickly dismount and crawl into our funkholes. From where I lie on the hill side I can see some of the bivouacs, one of which as I watch is smashed to the ground by a shell, but there is no explosion. Rushing to the remains of the shelter, careless of further shells, we find two forms struggling amongst the wreckage; if the shell had not been a dud these two would be no more. They had built their bivouac with a sunken floor which acted as a funk-hole.

The number of duds the enemy is sending over is ever increasing in number. Out of seven that dropped amongst our lines, three failed to explode. Not only are the Turkish shells becoming faulty but their firing is not so accurate; probably the gun barrels are wearing. If this be a true indication of the enemy resources it seems a possible sign that the end is coming. These things are interpreted by us as good omens, the first signs of light in what for years has been a very black sky. We talk to German prisoners about it, but they do not know much. Propaganda will always keep the actual truth hidden, they believe the Allies to be almost crushed in France and we are told that the reverse is the case.

Last week we had some fifty Germans through our hands whom we had taken in a raid the night before. At first they were sullen till we convinced them we were well disposed towards them. With the few who spoke English we exchanged the news of our respective bulletins. Ours merely told of actions and such of their results as it suited the High Command to divulge. With the Germans it was all of the nearness of the Allies' destruction, how Germany was gaining the upper hand and would soon crush us. We showed them our clothes, which were much better than their own; explained to the point of exaggeration how well we fared. They could not believe it, thinking we were far worse off.

They showed signs of doubting their own bulletins, then with sorrowful head-shaking, indicative of this doubt, gave us to understand that they must have been misled. It is all so much propaganda; we know, for it is used amongst us too.

We have read in papers from home of victories, we have been in these victories and know them to be something vastly different. It would not do to tell the general public otherwise; that is politics or, as it is termed these days, propaganda.

We read of German atrocities, of raping of women and ruthless devastation, the sort of published things which make men enlist. The papers are always full of such, of the frightful Hun and his *Kultur*. We have long since found out how wrong most of it is. The Hun is not, could not be, as bad as he is painted, but

170

CROSSING THE JORDAN AT GHORANIYEH BRIDGE-HEAD

FRIENDSHIP BETWEEN MAN AND HORSE. BOTH RESTING AFTER STUNT

if these gross exaggerations and untruths were not published the war would languish for lack of incentive. If the papers were to say how gentlemanly the enemy was and how well he treated our prisoners, people would say 'why do we fight him?' Certainly a foundation of truth is in a number of these accusations, the German has been guilty of a number of harsh actions, but are we so blameless that we are fit to condemn?

The Turk with his world-renowned reputation for cruelty has been more chivalrous to our prisoners than is generally credited. When he has been pushed back he has blown up wells but never poisoned them; he has laid mines and traps, but that is permissible in war. His treatment of prisoners perhaps is not of the best, but it could be very much worse and is better than the newspapers say. The Turk too has not reached the height of civilisation that Western countries have, so that his treatment is the more creditable for this.

I have come to know the Hun and found him far different from what we are led to believe. His courage is of no mean order and commands our utmost admiration. That we are opposed is but chance. We are told that he caused the war, that he hates England and has been brought up to look upon the British as his natural enemy, despite the fact that we are cousins. I have talked to Germans about this and they mostly agree in denial of any hatred for England; on the contrary they look upon us as relatives and had never expected that we would declare war against them. The secret of who caused the war is something we may know when it is all over, certainly now it seems obscure but more than likely the evil lay in treaties. Germany is allied to Austria and if that country chooses to accept a challenge in the Balkans, Germany is automatically drawn in.

If politicians had made different treaties, we might have been fighting with and not against Germany; it is all so much chance. In the eyes of the Supreme Being all men are equal? who are we that we should damn the Hun? To be a good soldier one should hate the enemy. Accepting this, then I am a bad soldier, and there are many more bad soldiers in this army though nevertheless there are many who hate him with a good and deep hatred; but I doubt if they know why. If our general opinion was taken it probably would reveal a good-natured tolerance for the Turk and an un-stinted admiration for the German, tinged perhaps with a little dislike. We fight them because that is why we are here, we are not concerned with the ethics of the thing. That it is the German and the Turk and the Austrian matters little, they are the enemy and farther than that we do not trouble; it could as easily be Russia or some other country we fight. No matter who it be we would do the job as we are doing now. We have never had contact with the enemy in pre-war days to learn to like or understand him so that we have no bias or opinion concerning him and fight him with an easy conscience.

The Germans on this front have been steadily increasing, since entering the valley we have felt their presence in growing numbers; all is not well either between them and the Turks. The former tolerate the Turks who are their ally but never fraternise with them, and in turn this toleration and Western overbearing are resented. From a batch of prisoners we took one night we learnt a peculiar story indicative of this growing ill-feeling.

The German, with typical overbearing, had criticised the Turk in action, who had suggested that the former by example do better; accordingly a German raid was planned with Turkish supports. The raid not meeting with the anticipated success, the Germans fell back on their supports, who, instead of supplying the assistance they were there to give, kept the Germans in the line, even going so far as to fire on them. Thus between two fires they chose us as the lesser evil and surrendered.

What the German is like on the Western front we do not know; here they are mostly technical units, Air Force and of late quite a deal of infantry. A small number serve artillery, though this chiefly is the function of the Austrians and Turks. The Germans opposed to us are a fine type, not at all the barbarian as people at home believe; their courage is superb, particularly the machine-gunners, who never vacate a position. Time and time again we have been held up by the dogged determination of these; they never give way even when they know that surrender would mean life, persistence death.

A few nights back we took some Turks in a raid but instead of placing them in the compound till sufficient were there to take back to Jericho, they were sent straight away in; six of them being given to me to escort. Passing over the bridge a loaf of bread came floating down stream. Without any hesitation, two of the prisoners floundered into the swiftly flowing water to obtain it whilst the remainder ran along the bank waiting to fight with those in the stream for possession when they waded ashore. As they secured the food I rode up and watched them wolf it down like wild men.

Continuing our way, they showed great interest in my clothes and horse, which one stroked with much timidity, whilst another ran his hand over my leggings. I could make nothing of their conversation, but by their gestures judged they were discussing the good clothes I wore and my appearance of well-being in sad contrast to their worn and shabby uniforms. It seemed beyond their understanding that I should be so well-clad and apparently so much better off in every way than they. I gave them each a cigarette which they acknowledged with much volubility and gestures of thanks. Realising that I intended them no harm they became like children, as indeed they are, and gambolled along the road resigned to the future and seemingly anticipating their coming incarceration without fear. They will in time find it a good exchange for their late bare existence as soldiers.

It was too late to return to the line after disposing of my charges so I rode across to a nearby cavalry detachment to sleep for the night, intending to return immediately after daylight.

At the first signs of morning light I was awakened by a droning overhead and a number of concussions. Quickly arousing myself I found three German planes coming towards us dropping bombs on the river bed.

Hurriedly I sought a fold in the ground as one plane, a little detached, flew in our direction; for of all war terrors nothing is more unnerving than a bomb, whose whine can be heard for several seconds before the explosion.

Flying low down this plane passed over us, then turned and came back. I could distinctly see the bomb in the rack, a very large one of a type we erroneously called aerial torpedoes. Its release was perfectly visible until the speed with which it travelled cloaked it with invisibility, then to my ears came the drone of its whirring body increasing in volume as it neared the ground, culminating in a belching burst of smoke and sound, so near that it seemed as if I was right under it. Immediately after the detonation I jumped to my feet seeking to find what damage had been done. As I did so to my ears came the squealing of wounded and dying horses. Rushing to the cavalry troop nearby, I found that one horse had escaped, most of them being killed, whilst a few men had also been injured. It cut my heart like a knife to see these suffering horses; what cavalryman wouldn't feel it? One poor animal struggling near so affected me that I drew my revolver and ended its misery. The shot was to me like a stab in my own flesh, for to kill a horse hurts far more than to do likewise to any German or Turk. Just one bomb had accounted for almost a full troop of horses. I cursed the departing plane; useless, I knew, but it relieved my feelings.

Soon our own airmen were up and after the bombers, and little white puffs appeared in the sky as the anti-aircraft shells burst. That these bombers would probably be caught and brought down by our own machines, quicker in pursuit than the lumbering bombers, was some consolation, but not enough.

I should, I suppose, have felt thankful I escaped myself from flying splinters, being so close; but I was so mad about the horses that I had no thought for aught but them, unless to satisfy my rage, I wished the enemy airman was near enough to put my hands on him, I felt I could have killed a dozen to satisfy my rage; but still—it is war.

On returning to our lines I found a new face in the troop, a man who had left us badly wounded long ago and had, we believed, been invalided home. On rushing up to greet him I used the name we had known him by, but he quietly informed me that he had changed it since being discharged. 'How else do you think I could be here?' he asked, 'since the man you call me is no longer fit for service, the only way I could get back again was to enlist under another name.'

He makes the third I know who has done this. It gives rise to an interesting problem—why men honourably discharged who have done their share should come back into it again? This particular fellow had often talked of what he would do if he could only get out of the army. All he desired was to escape, and yet when he had accomplished this he for some reason comes back. Why? His explanation was simply that he missed the fellows he had been associated with for so long. That in itself was probably the only reason he could think of, the motive under it, the psychology of his and others' actions in doing the same thing, the something in men which makes them return like homing pigeons to tempt fate anew is incomprehensible, eludes understanding.

Not one of us at some time that would not have given all we possessed, even a limb, to escape, and yet when the scene changes and immediate fear is past we act in contradiction to our earnestly professed intentions.

Looking at the problem from the beginning, what first brings us into the arena, all we Colonials are volunteers, here of our own free will; conscription does not exist for us; then why is it? I doubt very much if we can call it patriotism, though we are patriotic to the length of egotistical overbearing where our country is concerned. We think we come from the fairest place on earth, which perhaps too is nearly true, and should anything be said against it, even the poorest and meanest is sufficiently imbued with love of country to stand up for its fair name, irrespective of place or opponents. To deride our country or belittle either it or its people, is the greatest insult that can be offered.

If then it is not patriotism, which is the more doubtful when our insularity is considered, we are too far from this turmoil to feel but the eddies of the storm and have not our homeland at stake as has England, we must seek a further reason which probably lies in our ancestry; and it is very likely too that all Britishers, whether English or Colonials, are actuated by a similar urge. We are a free Empire and resent interference, we are essentially rovers and colonists as the far-flung Empire proves. To breed men who will rove, who will dare, who will carry the British flag to all corners of the earth, requires courage and unquenchable grit and determination. Granted we possess these attributes, then what is the power that propels these forces, makes them function and bring to fruition what otherwise may only be dreams? The force that sent men forth to find and populate new countries, and propagate in them the same breed that urged their habitation, and in turn supply other races to grow up and emulate the example. The only thing that could supply the vital spark to set burning the flame of conquest, whether over a foe or the elements, unknown countries or waters, obstacles which our natural instincts compel us to overcome or whatever else it be that has made us what we are, is the inherent love of adventure, in seeking which we never count the cost.

In this, I believe, lies the explanation why men lay down their pens and take up swords, whether they do it of their own free will as we, or whether conscription makes it incumbent on them to do so without waiting to see if they would of their own accord, which doubtlessly the great majority of Britishers could be expected to do. Throughout the ages war has always been invested with glamour, with a false halo of glory, false because it is wrong that we should kill each other, but a natural inclination nevertheless, else otherwise there never would have been any wars.

The declaration of war was greeted with cheers, not with tears; yet the very people who cheered knew that many of them were acclaiming their near demise; but they cheered for all that, which proves that they enter into the great adventure without counting the cost. Once in, something is required to keep up the spirit created and this we call enthusiasm. It is fed by accounts of the enemy's barbarity if in the case of a great nation, as now we are opposed to; if it had been a smaller one, an insurrection perhaps, the flame would have been fed with the need to strengthen the empire to overcome a canker in our midst or some such thing.

Whether war is an adventure is best judged by those who have tasted of it, and if the great numbers who have were to be asked the question they would find it difficult to deny that some suggestion of this nature did not underlie their reason for being there. That war is wrong we know, but how to overcome this wrong we do not know, for as long as humanity knows greed and lacks forbearance wars will continue. A soldier's life is divisible into two parts; when he is actually under fire and his life is something that may be snapped at any moment, and when he is removed from those fears, either enjoying leave or a spell behind the line.

With the former all suggestion of adventure disappears, for it is no adventure to look death in the face, and most of us have done so at some time, many on more than one occasion. But the spirit that so controlled our thoughts and actions, that automatically and seemingly without volition compelled us to change from quiet civilians to noisy soldiers, considers not the consequence. It is only when the clammy hand is upon us that we realise this, that we call ourselves fools to be here and only ask that we may live to make our escape. Our minds then are not normal, and we think and do abnormal things inspired by fear which even the bravest cannot escape. What has been in imagination becomes a dread reality, our temerity in being here must pay, no adventure is without its risks, that is why it is an adventure. When removed from the fears and again in safety we soon forget these horrors, or at least in part. We never can fully forget, they are too searing for that; but contact with them gone, we again find warmth in the sunshine and search for the lighter side of life which is our just compensation. It is the anticipated indulgences of a soldier's life, the irresponsibility and lack of worry and not a little hero worship, which create the glamour. The noble promises of our rewards, glowing accounts of stirring deeds, bright bemedalled uniforms and the fanfare that always accompanies war—all that makes for glory. These things are difficult for youth to resist, for we have not the maturity to go deeper into the underlying reaction and count the cost. The more I reason it the greater seems the certainty that, beneath our reasons and explanations, our floundering efforts to understand the spirit that controls our destinies, is that of adventure. No one can enjoy the high lights of towns, can indulge themselves in utter abandon with less thought and care than a soldier. His life holds two extreme contrasts, as opposite as possibly they can be. He moves from the valley of death itself to laugh and jest in a fashion that, if he were not a soldier, would be considered ridiculous; probably one extreme drives him to the other. Whether the risk of the first is compensated by the second is more than I know even now. What I do know is that a soldier's life possesses something that we cannot explain or understand, a something that brings us here and makes us do the things we do, that I have done and will continue to do; and should I escape this war, in all probability another would find me again in the ranks. That something, that driving-power, that force, that mental suggestion—call it what you will—is really nothing else but the lure of adventure, that calls men into war, and when they escape and get back home, makes them immediately turn their steps back again.

* * * * * * * *

Our present sector is a trench system sunk in a small eminence running in regular line with the river on the enemy side. If it were not for some stunted bushes ahead, we could see right across the valley from our trenches. These same stunted bushes would provide excellent cover for an on-creeping enemy, so that they require constant vigilance and night occupation.

Behind our trenches, and immediately across the river, a small hill rises perpendicularly-capped with a short trench, and used as an observation post. From here we can see all around the valley but the sun's rays are very striking and add to the discomfiture of its occupation.

Elevated up here I search around the valley and find plenty of interest, which somewhat compensates for the arduous nature of the duty. Away to the left rises Mussellaba, now known as Camel's Hump in honour of the Camel Corps' bravery in defending it. They had exhausted their ammunition but, rather than surrender, rolled the very stones of which the hill was composed down on to the enemy below, seeking their destruction, and crushing them in the attempt.

Far across the valley moves a Turkish patrol, I follow them with my telescope and as the nearby battery does not open, obtain the range from their spotter nearby and try sniping them. My first shot is without result; but the second makes the patrol move faster. A few more shots and they disappear up a gully. A second and large patrol comes into view from the opposite direction, at which our artillery open, not so disdainful of this target.

The fire of a Turkish battery attracts my attention, and following the sound I see a troop of our cavalry come beneath its hail. One shell, falling immediately at the feet of the leading section, blows it completely out of the picture. One of our sixty-pounders behind approximates the Turkish guns' position and opens on it. This in turn attracts their fire, bursting shrapnel uncomfortably close to our post so that we sink into the trench till they are finished. A little while and the firing ceases so that I again take up my observation and find the valley opposite temporarily deserted, but not quite. Away down towards the Dead Sea I can see a patrol of our horsemen secreted behind some bushes, not visible to the Turkish lines. I look at them a few times but as they seem to be still inactive I forget them. A little later a detachment of Turkish infantry comes out into the open. I watch them move over the flat, wondering why the artillery do not open on them but their hesitancy is soon explained. Our cavalry from behind the bushes have come into the open at the gallop. The Turks seek shelter behind such rises as the country offers and fire at the oncoming horsemen, but as they come near hoist a piece of white cloth instead. The cavalry do not stop but charge right up to and past them, cutting with their swords as they go. Why they do this I am too far off to see distinctly, and a telescope can only cover one of two separated parties at a time. Probably they resent the firing first and white flag after, or maybe they have been waiting to catch this particular detachment; but what does it matter?

Towards afternoon a patrol of Sikh Lancers comes through the lines hard by our post with a number of prisoners. The Turks fear these sons of Ind, and are mortally afraid of becoming their prisoners. Turkish officers tell their men that our Hindoos never take prisoners; it is only propaganda, but it serves a purpose, being directed to intimidate possible deserters. The Indians are rather awe-inspiring in appearance which lends colour to this belief.

* * * * * * * *

September, 1918. We have drawn our last plough through the dust, made our last patrol over the barren valley; tonight the first shells will pass over preluding the anticipated advance. Our little wicker hospital is being emptied of its fever patients, those with a temperature of one hundred or less being returned to the lines.

Apparently the Turk's delusion has been complete; the bulk of his army is concentrated here against us thinking we are many when in reality we are so few, our real strength being on the coast seemingly not suspected. The very part of his line that has been weakened is where our troops have been bolstered for the attack. It leaves our end of the task rather hazardous, with infinitely superior forces pitted against us, but it is some compliment that it should be so; we are the senior division of the front.

As darkness becomes complete those first shells go over. Probably eighteen miles away are the guns that fire them, but so great is the flash of their mouths and so terrific their roar that even at this distance the earth beneath us quivers and shakes. The explosions are distinctly audible, and the sky lurid with the glow as they pour their hell and annihilation upon the enemy lines. They are heavy-calibred guns, brought especially from France for this one night's bombardment, and are lined together in close proximity in true Western fashion.

An enthusiasm is apparent amongst us, if such a thing is possible in these circumstances, if one can take a joy in the killing of one's fellows. The bombardment we hear in itself signals the determination and strength behind the coming advance, it seems to sing victory as the shells pour over. Something of this determination has permeated to our deadened brains, creating this enthusiasm; we feel imbued with hope, for we have heard and done so much towards what will follow tonight's work that, no matter how weary we are, we strain as a horse at the bridle to plunge in and be amongst it; for the atmosphere is charged with that tremulous feeling of anticipation which is like excitement. We sense that we are the all-powerful and itch to go and be amongst it, as the Assyrians of old poured down *like the wolf on the fold*; that is how we feel. Never before has the war seemed so near its end, never before have we gone over with such strength behind us, never have we felt this elation, this hope, this determination that will smash and break all that bars its path; it is as if God has awakened from His long sleep to speed us forth to make an end. As the wrestler, who has strained till he feels his body weakening with the very exertion, strives to make one great and final burst of strength; so do we, who have been so tormented with the valley conditions, make this great effort, though our bodies can scarcely stand to the strain; yet it is no longer the body that matters, the soul, the heart and the will have charge and thrust us forward. But with this difference: the wrestler is weary to exhaustion because of his foe, we are weary because of conditions; and so is the enemy, but we are not weary through his efforts. tonight we are again the men we were a year past, before the valley consumed us; we live on our vitality, our innate determination, not on our actual bodily strength; we have the will and the idea which is everything; the will to win, the idea that nothing can stay us. With such to bear us forth we feel we must crush all ahead, and in addition we have an added incentive, for we believe that at long last we will avenge and pay the last respects of our dear dead high up above on that plateau who await our coming. Our division has dwelt .in this hell-built desolation throughout the summer; others have come and gone but only we have seen it through. We are thin and worn, rotten with disease, weakened by fever and privations; casualties too have taken their toll. Stunts before have meant just another juggle with fate and life. But now it is different; we will be rid of the valley, which in itself means much, but still more than this; we go forward, many of us to die we know, but we nevertheless go forward with the great hope, for we know that now at last we are the masters. The whip is in our hands, and ours to wield it, as indeed we will. The feeling that these thoughts create is sufficient, we care not about our bodily strength. We line out and mount our horses; then as the command comes, ride into the night and to our fate. We ride out to conquer.

* * * * * * * *

Up the hillsides we go, traverse the familiar goat paths, a few desultory shells bursting amongst us: but we are going upward. The task is more difficult than before though we have not the rain and cold to contend with; but we are not healthy now as we were then.

When at last we top the rise, screens are thrown out, on one of which I ride. My path takes me along a ridge top, difficult to scale; I dismount and clamber up on foot then coax Blackboy after me. Ahead I see a Circassian village, reminiscent of a previous venture when they had fired on our rearguard, which is no uncommon thing. They are hostile to us, we know, but as my path leads me through their village I must risk that.

I cannot help wondering what my reception will be as I ride down upon their village; the thought is not pleasant, but I have my rifle ready and cocked, and long ago I lost any squeamishness such as firing on these people might cause. Not more than thirty rude mud huts clustered together constitute their village. Coming amongst the dwellings I search for signs of life, but it is not till I am well amongst them that I see any of the people. In an open doorway stands a woman, fair of complexion and of robust build, a suckling child on her breast. She does not speak but just looks at me with sullen stare; otherwise no sign of life appears. I know every house is tenanted: I can feel the people's eyes staring at me through the chinks.

Against one hut I espy a pomegranate tree all laden down with fruit, ripened and most enticing to my starved stomach. I am determined to have some of them, irrespective of my lonely position, and accordingly pick as many as I can cram into my feed bags. By neither sign nor action does anybody interfere or acknowledge my action; I should not have cared if they did.

On a house apart from the others I see the Turkish Flag floating idly in the breeze, half curled about the mast as with dejection. Coming to the doorway flapping wide open, I peer inside, but it seems unoccupied; I am half inclined to take this flag but think better of it and pass on, to be met around the corner by a wandering Turkish soldier. I halt a minute and look him over; but he has nothing worth worrying about so I lean forward to ride on and leave him. He grasps my stirrup leather and makes it plain that he is my prisoner, but I do not want him and push him away. If I bring him in it means another mouth to feed and food is too scarce when a man has to carry his all upon him. He follows me at a distance till we come in sight of the main column then, deserting me, moves towards them with his hands uplifted.

The country opening out, the need for screens no longer exists; so I rejoin the column and ride in my accustomed place. Night drawing near, a line of outposts is thrown out and we halt till morning. Seeing a group of the supply column I walk towards them and find them examining a broomstick bomb. I have seen men do this before, so I quickly move away but not before I hear its explosion and the fragments flying. Fools are always to be found who will meddle with things of which they are ignorant; four lives now paid the penalty for curiosity.

A feature of the fortification of the country ahead is a number of short trenches at scattered intervals. They are fully manned and usually have a machine-gun with a German crew. These are like so many isolated forts barring our path. With morning, as we move on, we meet one of these; after a few shots it shows a piece of white cloth. We walk forward dismounted, with fixed bayonets, in full view of the trench occupants, accepting their surrender. For some reason unknown to us, when near them they turn their machine-gun on us, violating the white flag. No order is given, nor do we wait for one but plunge forward behind outstretched bayonets to gain the trench. A few seconds, bloody seconds, and it is finished; nor do we become burdened with prisoners.

Farther ahead a German machine-gun, secreted behind a stone sangar, bars our passage, sweeping all the territory to right and left so that the entire column is held up. Men go forward with grenades but they do not come back; others charge it on horseback but this too is useless. Again it is tried, the horsemen approaching from two directions this time to distract the gunners, but still with no avail and a few more lives are lost.

A mountain battery manned by Hindoos is brought up, the *Bing Boys* as we fondly term them. After the first salvo they stop to see the result, but the gun is still working. Again the battery fires, for at all costs this machine-gun must be silenced. I can distinctly see from where I lie, the flying fragments of stone from the sangar as the shells explode amongst them. The battery pauses, and for a second or more there is silence, then the gun resumes its staccato roar. The battery opens out again, and this time does not cease till the sangar is no more.

It seems to me a pity that such men should perish. They knew they could not escape except by surrender, which they would not do. They did not ask quarter, but just served their gun knowing it was death; one must admire these German gunners.

As we ride up I peer into the remains of the sangar. The gun is shattered with one of its crew spattered over it where he had died. A second is in pieces near by; they must have died a dozen times.

This obstacle removed, we swing away and come at the gallop down the hill, not entirely escaping the fire of other scattered trenches. At its base we charged along a gully to meet a detachment that almost might purposely have been left to await us. With no thought other than to be first into the town (Amman) now so near, the objective of our previous efforts up here and for the capture of which we had all striven, we pressed forward. This detachment barred our path; so upon them we rode, some of our number falling as we passed, but the Turks nevertheless going under us to be trampled by the flying heels of our galloping horses.

Again we are halted, this time by a machine-gun high above us on a hillside. As we pull in behind a knoll for cover, a figure with fixed bayonet comes careering madly down the hillside to the stone hut that harbours the gun. Its crew, temporarily occupied with us, do not perceive him till he is almost at the house; they have just time to fire only a few shots when he reaches the cover of the walls. We can distinctly see the figure creeping like a relentless shadow along the wall till it disappears around a corner. We sit breathlessly waiting to see what will be the end of this peculiar contest; a few minutes silence; we venture onward. No gun fires now; how it has been silenced we do not know, probably by a grenade.

Entering the village we gallop through, and find it already in the possession of another unit, but much close fighting still occurs. On foot we scour for the un-surrendered parties, mostly in the overlooking hills, who are firing down on us. Swinging around a corner we encounter a batch coming towards us. I am so near one that I do not stay to fire, resting content by kicking him in the belly as I pass. It is all very quick and nasty, at such times one does not think but acts to the prompting of instinct, for one's brain is never normal under such circumstances. We seek only to kill; not that we joy in that, but if we do not, it is we who will be killed; it is simply self-preservation. In things like this, little insignificant fellows become big men, men who ordinarily could not hurt a fly now kill with the utmost abandon, and take pride in doing it. It is the subconscious animal lying dormant in us that rises and dictates our actions.

Down an alley we go, figures flitting by. I use my rifle from the hip like a revolver. Men everywhere, ours and Turks, some of the latter seeking shelter till it is over, when they will crawl forth and surrender; others carry the battle to us.

Round a corner, I find myself in a backwash hemmed in by houses except for a narrow passage. It is a maze, I do, not know the geography of the town, nor care; really I do not know anything much, one never does at these times, everything is much a blur.

I see a party of Turks drop through a hole under a house, as I pass I give them a grenade for company. I do not hear its explosion nor do I wait to hear; but it will explode; anyway, there is so much noise.

In a surprisingly short time the din ceases, all is over before things seem to have properly begun. By dark we have the town, getting it far more easily than we expected. We have only the prisoners to gather in before pushing on again.

Three times have we assailed the plateau, each time with this town our objective; it has caused a lot of bitterness and suffering, so we feel great satisfaction in holding it now. That we have failed before has rankled, but at last the debt is paid.

The town nestles on the fork of two gullies, overshadowed by the hills rising on each side. Along the bed of one gully water flows, passing through and supplying the village. Cut into the hillside are the remnants of an ancient Roman amphitheatre, half of the structure still standing as a monument to its Roman builders. We walk amongst the ruins, awed by this evident might of an empire gone into decay.

Around a house cluster a few khaki-clad figures; two women are inside. But a little while ago these same men had no thoughts other than their duty as soldiers; yet in such manner is the human mind constructed that that task disposed of their mood softens as their feelings become actuated by this vision of femininity. The women in all probability belonged to the Turkish Ambulance stationed here Fair of skin, their nationality is doubtful, possibly of some Northern Palestine race. I did not speak to them, so I do not know. Seemingly they realise their effect on these miserable soldiers and are not averse to its consequences.

What kind of hospital has been located here we do not know. These are not the only women we have seen. Two more we found roaming the open country. They seemingly had tried to escape but a wandering patrol had come across them. Practically nude and half hysterical when found, they were either suffering from something that had happened, or else feared what might happen to lone women at the hands of roaming soldiers. Their fears of us were groundless nevertheless; the patrol supplied them with great coats and brought them in unharmed, mounted on their horses.

Somebody has found a body, or to be more exact the remains of one of our fellows, lost here early in the year. The flesh is stripped from the body and not a vestige of clothing remains. No identity disc hangs around the neck or rather where the neck should be, for the head has come apart. We have no means of telling who it could have been and stand pondering till someone notices a gold tooth. The head is picked up and passed along but nobody recollects the fillings. It may be from another squadron, so we tell others about it. Eventually somebody thinks he remembers and a little group stand around striving to remember a face suggested by a gold tooth. They talk and argue till finally they are satisfied. A cross will be erected with a name on it, a message will tell some wondering home that a son is dead, and uncertainty will cease. We find other bodies not so difficult to identify as this one, and bodies of fellows of whom we knew nothing; we had perhaps seen them fall and no more, or they had just disappeared and we thought them prisoners till the Turkish lists came through and their names were missing, and so they had become officially accounted as *Missing*.

* * * * * * * *

Our division has driven into this arm of the Turkish army like a wedge. The upper half, too numerous for us to cope with, are fleeing north, whilst the remainder have withdrawn south and are consolidating a redoubt at a railway station. Hemmed in on all sides, with Lawrence below, the Dead Sea to one and the desert to the other, and us forming a perfect stopper above, the Turks can please themselves about it; in the meantime we stay at the township awaiting developments.

Our present camping ground has previously been occupied by Turks and is swarming with vermin, so that we have taken to scratching more than ever. As I sit with my trousers removed, chasing the elusive little devils that bite my legs, a flock of goats come streaming over the hill top, in their wake a Hindoo artilleryman from one of the mountain batteries. Somebody calls our attention and quickly we go streaming up the hillside to get some of this meat.

Lenny running near me asks where are my army pants, I turn and see that except for his boots he is entirely unclothed. He grins at me as we both rush the same animal. Grasping it by the hind legs I struggle, and hold on till Lenny gets his rifle. Quickly we skin the animal and hack out the warm chops with our bayonets; they are rough chops but food for all that, and fresh too.

The Indian in the meantime has become quite concerned, thinking to lose his promised feast, but we soon appease him by rounding up some of the goats and leading them to him, the Bedouin owner standing by and gesticulating, saying a lot in his own language, which troubles us very little, for he will be compensated by the Government.

The Indian bows and offers his thanks, then disappears over the hill, dragging his struggling dinner behind much to our amusement. Religion is a devil of a business when it stands in the way of one's belly like this. We would have killed and skinned them for him, only his creed will not permit his contamination by our contact with his meat.

This is a matter which makes it very difficult to fully use the Hindoos, for they must have their meat alive with them and kill it according to the rites of their faith, and at times it is not easy to keep up this meat supply.

Our more than welcome meat dinner disposed of, we seek for the makings of a cigarette. I manage to scrape sufficient from my pockets, tobacco that I had taken from prisoners, but others are less fortunate. I have no papers, only a piece of Turkish newsprint all heavy with ink. I have been using this for some days, so that my skin is yellowing with the jaundice, but that cannot be helped. One must smoke and when the necessary materials are not available we must use what are.

After today I too will be reduced to smoking what I can as others around me do now. Some use tea or ground leaves from trees, things to which I am no stranger. Before today we have been reduced to such, and even to horse manure. Our taste is much depraved, and we have often eaten and drunk things quite as bad in their way.

A formation of our planes goes over, flying south to the Turkish position, a quantity of bombs slung underneath. Each day they do that to hasten the Turks' capitulation, for the open country will not permit of our too close approach. This daily bombing will gradually wear them down and they must run short of food too; they cannot forage, our daily patrols see to that.

* * * * * * * *

Today the patrol squadron reported a white flag over the redoubt and now we go south to see about it; we have been waiting for just this. Half-way we pass the Turkish commander coming north under escort, a little fellow like most Turks and looking very glum, as is only natural.

Night is falling as we draw near, but it is still light enough to permit us a view of this redoubt in which we are so keenly interested. Here lies the flower of the Ottoman army, some five thousand or more strong, whereas we a bare thousand.

Built around the station, at which stands a train, little is noticeable of the trenches till we are very close. Constructed so that as much as possible is below the ground, and thus the more impervious to all attack, except aerial bombs. The station is of the fortified type, common in this wild country, of stone structure with gridded windows and rifle ports along the walls and doors of steel. These little forts are in peace time especially built to fight off the Bedouins who have a kink for attacking trains for plunder.

By arrangement the Turks are to remain fully armed till morning, as they fear the Bedouins may attack them during the night; they hate each other—though both of Islam; the former too has for long years twisted his heel into the desert dweller's neck, who craves nothing better than to repay a little. This

190

gives rise to a rather peculiar position, the like of which none of us have ever before known, and because of it, should the Turk change his mind during the night and attack, we would be in an awkward predicament, being much outnumbered and exposed. In the end it would avail him little, for more troops are above us, but that is of little comfort to us here.

It is agreed that we throw a line of posts around one half of the redoubt, the Turk having the balance to guard, thus effectually keeping the Bedouins out. They are about us in goodly numbers, on horse and on foot, like so many vultures consumed with hunger awaiting their prey. The Turkish fear of this fate so near them is quite understandable when one considers how they have always maltreated and done their utmost to suppress them.

This feeling between Turk and Arab reveals an interesting fact that we have but recently discovered, and a highly significant one too. That through the long campaign the Arabs have taken approximately 17,000 Turkish prisoners whereas the Turks have not taken a single Arab. To the Arab the Turk is an enemy in arms, but to the Turk the Arab is a rebel, and deserving of a rebel's fate.

We get little chance to sleep through the night. Turks constantly come amongst us for water from the well which we have taken the precaution to hold; bullets too are flying broadcast. The sky is repeatedly lit up with the countless flares the Turks are continually firing, to which is added the din of rifles and machine-guns, all fired to keep the Turkish courage up and intimidate the Bedouins.

Hearing a chewing noise I find on investigation that Blackboy has gnawed his martingale whilst the horse next him has industriously removed half his tail; this is the second time since I have had him that this has occurred. I muzzle Blackboy, also the horses on either side of him; we carry contraptions for this purpose. The poor hungry beasts will eat anything.

Wearily and eerily the night drags on. I have given up hope of any sleep, and lie on my back for greater security from flying fragments, smoking endless cigarettes made from tobacco I have just become possessed of *per media* of prisoners. I cannot help thinking of the incongruity of our present position. Enemies both, only a few days ago at each others' throats, and now in mutual agreement we perform outposts side by side awaiting morning so that one can surrender to the other.

When at last day does break we are up and about our work of gathering in all the Turks ensconced in the redoubt. Our troops coming to a machine-gun ride up to its very snout and gather in the crew. They watch us coming, with their gun trained in our direction,—one press of the button enough to blow us to hell! So on it goes; post after post is lined up and disarmed, then marched to one huge group which is slowly assembling. We walk amongst and mix with them like friends, the souvenir-collector in his glory with everything from a rifle to a train at his disposal.

Hitching Blackboy to a car-buffer I wander amongst the trenches, searching for what I don't know, moving more from curiosity than with determined intent. Coming to a tent I pause as I am about to enter, arrested by a stench, the smell of putrefying flesh. Pulling the flap aside I peer in and find a group of decomposing bodies, their bellies swollen, stretching their clothes to grotesque size. One in his shirt only sprawls awkwardly with his entrails passing out, as is common with bodies left in the heat. The smell is too much, and I move on to another tent, to find the same again. Scattered about the ground in odd places are others in similar condition, whilst back at the station I find a fatigue party composed of Turks removing more bodies from the building.

They lie inside in heaps quite clearly visible through the doorway. Some plainly have died of their wounds or been killed, but these are very few; the greater number have no marks upon them. From a medical sergeant hurrying by I learn it is either typhus or cholera, he is not sure which. No wonder with this scourge amongst them they had surrendered; that in itself was sufficient reason irrespective of our dominance.

One of our planes goes by overhead; I can distinctly see the bombs in the racks underneath; we have spoiled his day for him, for he did not expect to find us in occupation. A coloured streamer flutters down with a message attached.

We find much to do; it takes all day to clean up the redoubt; the sick and wounded must be cared for and the prisoners got away. Those able to walk set out under escort on the long trail to our back lines. Thousands of rifles have been dumped in heaps, and countless quantities of ammunition and equipment too. All this must be gathered and moved out, which will be facilitated as we now hold the roadway. The task of escort is no light one; one can see the prison line stretching as far as the eye can reach, and many hundreds have not yet joined in. A feeling of exultation is in the air, a suggestion of the gradual breaking up of the Turkish resistance; success to our efforts seems growing till we almost dare to believe that victory is in the air.

I follow the prisoners back, and half-way I stand on a rise and can see neither beginning nor end of the long serpentine line stretching across east and west. A little farther we pass a dead body propped up against some rocks with a cigarette hanging from its mouth, someone's ribald wit at a corpse's expense—but we have long since ceased to find anything to inspire respect for death, it is too common. A man ahead rides over to it, probably attracted by what looked like a prospective smoke, but it was only a paper tube with no tobacco core.

Back at the town we captured some days previously we find much to occupy us in the necessary cleaning up. Turks are continually appearing from nowhere, anxious to give themselves up and probably fearing to be caught by the nomads. We are sick of them, one finds them everywhere. It has been difficult to feed us before we acquired all these prisoners; now it is still more so for our rations have to be shared. We receive about half our issue, which is less than enough to exist on, so that perforce we must turn to the country more industriously than ever. Such sheep and goats as we find quickly disappear. At every opportunity we search the prisoners for tobacco and papers; I have some of each now but I am still bright and yellow.

We hear the first rumours of the unqualified success of the push, that the other divisions of our corps are flying north, unrestrictedly sweeping all before them; we wonder if we will join in.

The town cleared, we back-track to the valley, following in line with the snakelike stream of prisoners now some eleven thousand in number. They are for ever falling with broken feet and sickness, and the escort curse and blaspheme at their task. We jeer them on and laugh at their discomfiture, for we have ever made light of each other's troubles.

Anything suggestive of food by the wayside creates a rush and struggle amongst this distressed, half-starved rabble, full of sickness and soreness. Their clothes are worn and many are without boots, substituting puttees wrapped around their feet. One sees many of them hoisted up on the saddles of their guards, who though they outwardly are disdainful and curse them, are nevertheless very sorry for their pitiable condition, doing what they can to alleviate it.

We top the valley as the sun is sinking to rest, and to my wearied brain, half-dormant through lack of sleep, and to my numb senses, comes an extraordinary hallucination.

Since first we set foot in Palestine our path in varying degrees has been dogged by the inevitable dust. Initially it greeted us on the border and for months made life wretched by its vagaries. For a time during our hectic rush up the coastal plains we were comparatively free, but later it returned with greater intensity as we entered the valley. Here, through the long summer months, it has never for an instant subsided, becoming so much a part of our daily lives that we had almost grown used to its irritation.

Now, as we ride down into the valley from the plateau it is stirred in great clouds, hanging suspended in the air like a gigantic pall, turned to redness resembling a sea of blood by the fiery rays of the setting sun. Through it are visible the prisoners and their escort as they pass across the plain below. Such are the tricks that nature plays that the heat-waves moving as they do in a mirage, give the fantastic effect of prisoners and escort indulging in combat as their refracted images flicker in the dazzle. As I stare, so real is the illusion that this dust, which actually is greyish black, seems bloody by the glitter of the sun. We almost seem to be swimming in its redness.

My mind runs backwards through the vicissitudes we have known, visualising the sorrows and horrors of war; everywhere is blood, everything is tinged with blood. The pall is like a picture sheet on which appears the past in a kaleidoscopic jumble made real, or perhaps conjured up, by this vision of marching men below. So real does it seem that my attention, focused and held as by a hypnotic spell, is only distracted when, as we ride lower into the valley, I turn my head from the blinding glare of the passing sun and ride a few moments with closed eyes. Only then does the vision pass, and instead of a battlefield seething in blood I see the undistorted images as they really are, prisoners and escort passing through a cloud of dust made red by the setting sun—red dust.

My thoughts wandering in the past, I think how much dust has been an integral part of our daily lives and existence. Think too of the blood that has been spilled upon it, both of enemy and Allies. Amongst it many have found manhood, many have been maimed and wrecked, it has seen the moulding of many characters, and too much misery and suffering and death. Even in the desert the sand storms were little different from the dust clouds. Much blood has run amongst it, tainting it red, so that perhaps what I saw in hallucination is more than a little true; it is red dust.

This is a country of dust made red by the deeds of full-blooded soldiery, struggling for life and existence and an ideal, spilling not a little of their life stream amidst the dust from which they sprang and to which they return—for we are told that from dust we come and by the addition of blood are permitted as mortals to live our allotted span, before disintegration returns us to that from which we sprang.

Through the centuries from the beginning of time, nations have fought over this very land across which we now move. The people of the Bible: Egyptians, Phoenicians and Romans, then later the Franks and Crusaders and followers of the Prophet, till the time of Napoleon; and now we British and a host more. All have lived and fought and died, bleeding in the dust of which they were made, making it as are they—red dust. Always throughout time it has been the same. Soldiers, what are we? Just a little dust, made animate with blood to struggle and die, pouring out the precious liquid of life to become dust again: as in life, so in death. Dust, red dust.

* * * * * * * *

We pass through the valley into the foothills and spend the night in the same place from where we first saw the Jordan many weary months ago. It is but fitting that from here we should make our last farewells, as long ago we first knew this hell upon earth, the Jordan Valley. It is with great sadness I take my last look upon this place of regrets, teeming with sorrows and memories. As I turn to mount my horse and ride on, my last look reveals the Mount, where, according to the Bible, Christ was tempted, and I pause and wonder what is the great secret, the power above which we call God. I understand religion now less than ever.

We are a silent column as we ride up amongst the hills, each of us has his thoughts and I think they are all as are mine—of the comrades left behind amongst the dust.

Long ago a prophecy was made that not till water flowed in the desert would the Holy Land be free of the unchristian yoke. As we come down into the plain country below Jerusalem we stop to water our horses, and the water in the troughs comes by pipe-line from Egypt, painfully laid behind our advancing army. So is the prophecy proved, and knowing of it we pause and think, for all is not well with the Turk, so that for which we have been hoping may at last be coming true—the end.

We ride into the old camp of last year, sick and weak through the stress and privations of the past months. We wonder if we shall be taken north to join in with our sister divisions in their glorious onward surge. Though worn and ill, we half hope for this, for it is our right to be there. However, it is not to be, for we soon learn that we have been placed in *C* class. It is so simple to say but what an awful lot it means. To be graded as *unfit* tells a story of the valley and its conditions that words cannot do.

We have little to do except attend to the usual fatigues, which are rather heavy with mounted men. We laze about, finding what amusement we can, talking and discussing the latest bulletins as they come through. We hear that Damascus has fallen and still the Turk retreats, headlong in his flight, leaving all behind him, oblivious to everything but his panicky urge to keep ahead of our pursuing legions.

This all indicates a radical change on the front; that it may mean the end we wonder, deep in our hearts we hope; but we say little.

Still more news filters through; the Turk is demoralised and flees without thought or order, consumed only by his mad desire to escape his fate. We hear of a column caught in a ravine and blown to hell by machine-guns and bombs, the place a shambles in the full sense of the word. It all serves to make his passage the fleeter.

At last we hear that Bulgaria has laid down the sword; this means a great deal because of its reaction on Turkey.

We groom and feed our horses with greater freedom from care than we have known for years. The thought of new country has always held an appeal for us, and we hope to see the cities to the north that are daily falling like ninepins, Damascus, Aleppo and others. Things are happening so quickly that we become bewildered in the train of events, each day bringing something new.

One day we hear that the advance has exhausted itself; our corps cannot push forward any more, they have outstripped their supplies and are worn out with the rapid pursuit. Despite this the Turk still flees north, and if our horses cannot any longer follow, the Air Force can.

At last we hear, we have half expected it for days. Turkey has fallen in the dust of her retreat, and passed to the limbo of defeated nations.

A CAMEL TRAIN ON THE DESERT

ENGLISH 18-POUNDER BATTERY

Conjecture is rife: we ask will we go to France, or will we continue through the Balkans to Austria and so create a new front? That Germany may be on the borderland of collapse is something we have not fully appreciated. And that it is possible we could penetrate to Austria is due in an immeasurable degree to the individual efforts, whether direct or indirect, of T. E. Lawrence. His constant harrying of the Turkish flank depleted the actionable forces available against us until victory was finally achieved.

It is night; we lie in our bivouacs, talking or playing cards, when our attention is attracted by a flare bursting over Headquarters. It is not long before the news has spread and passed along—The Armistice!

We half doubt it, though official. No great elation is shown, no cheering or noise, we take it calmly and return to our shelters. The day has been so long coming, we are perhaps too numbed to appreciate all it means. We have known so much that is sad and full of sorrow, and many joys, too. Our mentalities have been so stretched from extremes and we have seen so many things, that the gift of spontaneous enthusiasm seems to have become atrophied.

It was now that a most unfortunate incident occurred, though one not to be wondered at; it was surprising indeed that it had not happened before. The protection afforded the lowly and degenerate Arabs this side of the Jordan, ever so apparent, which they, a cunning race, have always been quick to perceive and exploit to the extreme could have but such an ending.

The natives of Surafend, a nearby village, notorious for thieving and worse, had grown more audacious with the probable realisation that soon we would pass on for ever. At night they would sneak amongst the lines, pilfering and robbing unchecked as we had no redress, the High Command being seemingly unwilling to punish their depredations.

One night a New Zealander was roused from sleep by an Arab from this village foraging amongst the belongings beneath his head. Shouting to the horse-picket, he gave chase, to be shot in his tracks and found, by the upcoming picket, dead. This happening, which was not the first such death, reached the high pinnacle of restraint and became the more aggravated as no definite action was taken by the Authorities despite demands that long-delayed justice should be meted out.

After a day of organising, a cordon was thrown around the village in the early night. Women and children were passed out, and then, armed mostly with sticks, the men entered the village and dealt out to the villagers their long overdue deserts, ending by firing the thatched huts, whilst we, the balance of the division, and our Scotch and English artillery, stood by in approval and in some cases lending active support.

The conflagration being visible at Headquarters, a battalion of English infantry was despatched to quell the disturbance. But they too had smarted at Arab hands, and were by no means willing to be used against comrades-in-arms, and so commenced a counter-demonstration on their own.

This action, it must be remembered, had its root in more than the recent murder. It was, in fact, traceable to the ill-feeling due to Headquarters' deliberate omission to act in previous instances. This affair only added the last straw, breaking the restraint of men angry beyond normal reasoning.

The night over, morning saw many dead and injured Arabs, and also a return to order of the men concerned, who anticipated disciplinary retaliation and were prepared to abide by it and take their punishment, but who were instead lectured in ill-considered fashion, which was unfortunate as coming from such a quarter, leaving a division of loyal men upset.

The Jews from Wady Hanein and Richon le Zion visited us for days in deputations of thanksgiving for having removed what had always been to them a source of terror and trouble, and done something which apparently they had lacked the courage or determination to do themselves long before.

****

The fates have heaped many sorrows upon us but have reserved for the last the cruellest of all, with true satanical humour, giving us the Armistice with one hand and robbing us of a great possession with the other. This cursed country is so impregnated with disease that the horses cannot be taken out, excepting a few of the best that will go to India and Egypt for military and police work; the remainder are lost.

Because of this today is very sad for me. I have lost many good friends, true and staunch comrades, and have mourned and sorrowed for their loss. Now I must lose Blackboy, the greatest and truest of all.

It had always been my dream that if we both lived I would bring him home and turn him out for the rest of his days with a paddock to himself. Some place where I could see and talk to him and feel his velvet muzzle in my hand; but alas for dreams!

He is but an animal, yet man never had truer friend. His condition is not good for he has been in the War since 1914 and his belly is full of sand. Even if he was amongst those to continue in military service, I would not let him pass into other hands; nor do I think he would want to. Never to know where he is or what he is doing and if he is well cared for—I could not bear it.

I have thought about it through the night and decided. The horses which are useless, that have cracked up, are to be destroyed first. They will be taken away and shot, then disembowelled for the jackals to do what we could not. Burial would be impossible, to leave them would cause disease.

When the condemned horses from our regiment go out today, Blackboy will be amongst them, as too I think will be many another's much-loved horse. That he should provide a meal for the scavenging jackal is abhorrent and loathsome in the extreme, but it cannot be avoided, there is no other path.

Poor reward for patient service, but it is this or leave him and never know what becomes of him. To think of him pining, as I know he would, or perhaps being ill-treated! If he is shot it will be painless and he will never know unnecessary suffering. It is best.

Taking him off the line in the early morning I walk with him away from the camp. I cannot saddle or ride him on this his last day of life, we are friends, not man and beast. I do not even bridle him; as I walk away he follows alongside with his head near my shoulder. I talk to him and tell him how I feel, stroke his muzzle and feed him with a little sugar I have stolen for him. He nuzzles my hand; it isn't only the sugar, he likes the feel of my flesh; it is his way of showing affection.

It is mid-afternoon when we return, the time set down for the condemned horses to go; I have had these last few hours with him. When a man has been through what we two have together, he does not look upon his horse just as an animal. He is far more than that, he is one's best friend. No true cavalryman ever placed himself before his mount, and I love him, as indeed most of us do.

The Remounts, whose task it is to destroy these horses, are here now to take them. I put my arms around old Blackboy's neck and kiss him, feeling his muzzle against my cheek. That there are tears in my eyes does not shame me. I give him a last pat and a little bit of sugar and watch his sleek black form, now thin and emaciated, as he is led away. He is gone.

I leave the lines and walk by myself to the same spot we two had gone this morning. I sit and think till it is dark. It is over now, he is no more.

I feel a void in my heart for I had loved him. I have done what I think best, he has passed out of my life but not from my memory, and knew nothing about it. No suffering; he will be at peace and though my heart will never forget him, I know where he is and that no one else will ever ride or ill-treat him.

The Armistice has brought joy but also much sadness for many of us. Others have to part with the horses they loved; I see more than one wet eye amongst my fellows.

****

The moon beams upon the empty desert sands, sands I once hated, now they seem almost friendly. My thoughts project into them and are mirrored back in living images like a mirage. Through my mind pass memories of the weary bygone months spent here, now turning into years. In passing away from it all, I picture not the hardships but the friends I have had. Memories come in a jumble interspersed with regrets and not a little sadness.

So real are they that perhaps I half dream. The noise of the rattling train, the presence of three figures lying huddled on the floor of the truck are non-existent. My mind, my heart, my soul is out there, there in the desert. Memories press in upon me and weigh me down with their realism. I see things that I had hardly thought of before.

How often that for which we live and strive becomes as nothing when we possess it. I have lived, or rather existed for what seems ages, awaiting today, the day I should go home. Now it is here it means nothing; it is as ashes. Just to pick up one's belongings and line out for the last time—it seemed so easy and desirable. The thought so enwraps one that we forget, or do not think, of the heart-tugging it will mean.

I had thought myself fortunate in leaving ahead of the regiment, in taking an opportunity that presented itself. How much that regiment has become to me, how much the friendships behind mean to me, I now know.

Some scattered little white crosses—all that is left of a faithful horse—memories of days and nights spent with these that are no more—all these things flash past my imaginary vision out in the desert. These sands I may never see again; had thought I had never wished to, how they fascinate now—they are more than I have ever understood.

It is here that manhood has come. I have jumped the period of youth, it is somewhere amongst this wilderness, given for a cause. The desert that has always seemed so unfriendly, that has kept us ever at a distance, has a lure that one does not realise till leaving it. The body will pass out and away from it, but a little corner of the mind will always be devoted to its memory. Something of us all will be left behind.

The star-spangled sky that always is so low. It has seen and knows, it smiles that we think we can escape or ever forget the years spent beneath its canopy. That I ever shall forget I doubt;

some day the magnetism will become too strong, I will tread these places again; they grip my heart too firmly to avoid.

Faces appear to me, faces of friends that are gone, whose bones lie out in the open, friendships such as one will never know again, blood brotherhoods. I see them as we were together, as we lived, as they died.

Greatest friend of all, old Blackboy. He looks at me half in sadness, half in joy. I tell him I did it for the best, a poor reward for a great service but the best I could bestow. It was painless to him; to me always a regretful memory. I owe you my life more than once, faithful friend!

I picture Smith, gone where, only God knows. I have never heard of him since that morning in the valley when his brain snapped.

Where now is the glamour and the glory? It is a sham. We were heroes, nothing was too good, promises were easy; now it is all over, will people forget? The dread is gone, the world is safe from autocratic kings, democracy will rule. But what of those who made it possible, who have given their all in sacrifice, whose bodies and minds are shattered? Will they be forgotten and sink into oblivion, whilst the usurper at their desks takes what they have forfeited for patriotism?

What of those who have given their youth, who went away smiling boys and came back hardened men? Will the world allow for the fire that has twisted their souls? Will it make allowances or will it expect the same ability as from the man who never left his home shelter? If the years torn from his life at times make labour difficult, will the world bear with him?

The shams, the pomps, the hypocrisy and endless deceits of war are gone; the task is accomplished and their need no longer exists. From the froth and effervescent enthusiasm which has brought us here we will sink into a niche in a mundane world.

Patriots have talked of the glory of war, a holy cause; there is no glory in war, only pain, suffering, and delusion.

I sink down and dream, dream that I ride across the Jordan Valley on Blackboy. Ride for the last time through the dust, the red, red dust. Friends are about me, real friends. The hypocritical world with its false values and greed are behind, far behind. Here is peace in a world peopled with friendly faces that I know. It is not that 1 fear the other battle ahead still to be fought, the battle of life, it is that I am saying good-bye to something that many of us have never known—our youth.

LEONAUR

ALSO FROM LEONAUR
AVAILABLE IN SOFTCOVER OR HARDCOVER WITH DUST JACKET

WAR BEYOND THE DRAGON PAGODA by *J. J. Snodgrass*—A Personal Narrative of the First Anglo-Burmese War 1824 - 1826.

ALL FOR A SHILLING A DAY by *Donald F. Featherstone*—The story of H.M. 16th, the Queen's Lancers During the first Sikh War 1845-1846.

AT THEM WITH THE BAYONET by *Donald F. Featherstone*—The first Anglo-Sikh War 1845-1846.

A LEONAUR ORIGINAL

THE HERO OF ALIWAL by *James Humphries*—The days when young Harry Smith wore the green jacket of the 95th-Wellington's famous riflemen-campaigning in Spain against Napoleon's French with his beautiful young bride Juana have long gone. Now, Sir Harry Smith is in his fifties approaching the end of a long career. His position in the Cape colony ends with an appointment as Deputy Adjutant-General to the army in India. There he joins the staff of Sir Hugh Gough to experience an Indian battlefield in the Gwalior War of 1843 as the power of the Marathas is finally crushed. Smith has little time for his superior's 'bull at a gate' style of battlefield tactics, but independent command is denied him. Little does he realise that the greatest opportunity of his military life is close at hand.

THE GURKHA WAR by *H. T. Prinsep*—The Anglo-Nepalese Conflict in North East India 1814-1816.

SOUND ADVANCE! by *Joseph Anderson*—Experiences of an officer of HM 50th regiment in Australia, Burma & the Gwalior war.

THE CAMPAIGN OF THE INDUS by *Thomas Holdsworth*—Experiences of a British Officer of the 2nd (Queen's Royal) Regiment in the Campaign to Place Shah Shuja on the Throne of Afghanistan 1838 - 1840.

WITH THE MADRAS EUROPEAN REGIMENT IN BURMA by *John Butler*—The Experiences of an Officer of the Honourable East India Company's Army During the First Anglo-Burmese War 1824 - 1826.

BESIEGED IN LUCKNOW by *Martin Richard Gubbins*—The Experiences of the Defender of 'Gubbins Post' before & during the sige of the residency at Lucknow, Indian Mutiny, 1857.

THE STORY OF THE GUIDES by *G.J. Younghusband*—The Exploits of the famous Indian Army Regiment from the northwest frontier 1847 - 1900.

LEONAUR

ALSO FROM LEONAUR
AVAILABLE IN SOFTCOVER OR HARDCOVER WITH DUST JACKET

WELLINGTON AND THE PYRENEES CAMPAIGN VOLUME I: FROM VI-TORIA TO THE BIDASSOA *by F. C. Beatson*—The final phase of the campaign in the Iberian Peninsula.

WELLINGTON AND THE INVASION OF FRANCE VOLUME II: THE BIDAS-SOA TO THE BATTLE OF THE NIVELLE *by F. C. Beatson*—The second of Beatson's series on the fall of Revolutionary France published by Leonaur, the reader is once again taken into the centre of Wellington's strategic and tactical genius.

WELLINGTON AND THE FALL OF FRANCE VOLUME III: THE GAVES AND THE BATTLE OF ORTHEZ by *F. C. Beatson*—This final chapter of F. C. Beatson's brilliant trilogy shows the 'captain of the age' at his most inspired and makes all three books essential additions to any Peninsular War library.

NAVAL BATTLES OF THE NAPOLEONIC WARS *by W. H. Fitchett*—Cape St. Vincent, the Nile, Cadiz, Copenhagen, Trafalgar & Others

SERGEANT GUILLEMARD: THE MAN WHO SHOT NELSON? *by Robert Guillemard*—A Soldier of the Infantry of the French Army of Napoleon on Campaign Throughout Europe

WITH THE GUARDS ACROSS THE PYRENEES by *Robert Batty*—The Experiences of a British Officer of Wellington's Army During the Battles for the Fall of Napoleonic France, 1813.

A STAFF OFFICER IN THE PENINSULA *by E. W. Buckham*—An Officer of the British Staff Corps Cavalry During the Peninsula Campaign of the Napoleonic Wars

THE LEIPZIG CAMPAIGN: 1813—NAPOLEON AND THE "BATTLE OF THE NATIONS" *by F. N. Maude*—Colonel Maude's analysis of Napoleon's campaign of 1813.

BUGEAUD: A PACK WITH A BATON by *Thomas Robert Bugeaud*—The Early Campaigns of a Soldier of Napoleon's Army Who Would Become a Marshal of France.

TWO LEONAUR ORIGINALS

SERGEANT NICOL by *Daniel Nicol*—The Experiences of a Gordon Highlander During the Napoleonic Wars in Egypt, the Peninsula and France.

WATERLOO RECOLLECTIONS by *Frederick Llewellyn*—Rare First Hand Accounts, Letters, Reports and Retellings from the Campaign of 1815.